PICKIN'
COTTON
on the way to
CHURCH

PICKIN' COTTON
on the way to
CHURCH

The LIFE *and* WORK *of*
FATHER BONIFACE
HARDIN, OSB

NANCY VAN NOTE CHISM

Indiana Historical Society Press | Indianapolis 2019

Printed in the United States of America

This book is a publication of the
Indiana Historical Society Press
Eugene and Marilyn Glick Indiana History Center
450 West Ohio Street
Indianapolis, Indiana 46202-3269 USA
www.indianahistory.org
Telephone orders 1-800-447-1830
Fax orders 1-317-234-0562
Online orders @ http://shop.indianahistory.org

The paper in this publication meets the minimum requirements of American National Standard for Information Sciences—Permanence of Paper for Printed Library Materials, ANSI Z39. 48–1984 ∞

Library of Congress Cataloging-in-Publication Data

Names: Chism, Nancy Van Note, author.
Title: Pickin' Cotton on the way to church : the life and work of Father Boniface Hardin,
    OSB / Nancy Van Note Chism.
Description: Indianapolis : Indiana Historical Society Press, 2019. | Includes biographical
    references and index.
Indentifiers: LCCN 2018024470 (print) | LCCN 2018039447 (ebook) | ISBN 9780871954343
    (epub) | ISBN 9780871954336 (cloth : qalk. paper)
Subjects LCSH: Hardin, Boniface, 1933-2012. | Monks—United
    States—Biography. | Benedictines—United States—Biography. | African
    American college presidents—Indiana—Biography. | Martin Center—History. | Martin
    University—History. | LCGFT: Biographies.
Classification: LCC BX4705.H1398 (ebook) | LCC BX4705.H1398 C45 2018 (print) | DDC
    271/.102 [B] —dc23
LC record available at https://lccn.loc.gov/2018024470

Sister Jane Edward Schilling
the Woman behind the Man

Pickin' Cotton on the Way to Church: The Life and Work of Father Boniface Hardin, OSB was made possible through the generous support of Michael G. Browning, Nancy and Grady Chism, John R. Goss, Michael and Kathryn Miller, Wayne and Susan Schmidt, and Dr. and Mrs. Gene E. Sease

Contents

Foreword

As the three brothers of Reverend Boniface Hardin, we welcome this biography. In 1933, our older brother, the subject of this work, was born as James Dwight Randolph Hardin in Louisville, Kentucky. He spent his early years in Bardstown, Kentucky, a historic small community thirty miles south of Louisville. In his formative years he lived with his parents Albert A. and Elizabeth Hardin. In 1938 William A. Hardin was born, followed in 1945 by Albert T. Hardin. In 1948 John A. Hardin was born and the family moved to Louisville. All of this is to inform you that as his brothers, we knew Randolph (later known as Boniface) as a unique person reflective of a Christian upbringing during a period in the United States when racial discrimination was legal and practiced daily.

As this book details, we know that in his Kentucky years Randolph (as his mother called him) often experienced racially defined slights from white Roman Catholics whom he still respected despite their unchristian behaviors. His faith in God kept him and his family going forward. His family members and colored (black was not acceptable at this point) Catholics in Bardstown and Louisville hoped that his presence in the seminary could open doors traditionally closed to blacks seeking to become priests. They shared scarce personal funds to help him defray the costs of his education at Saint Meinrad. After many years of study and prayer, he was finally ordained a Catholic priest in 1959. For Kentucky Catholics of color in Louisville and Bardstown, this was a moment of celebration to see one of their own receive a clergy rank held by very few black men in the United States.

Although most of his life was lived in Indiana, the Kentucky side of Randolph/Boniface Hardin reveals that he experienced love from his biological family members, including his two parents, we three brothers, aunts, uncles, and many cousins from coast to coast. His Kentucky years included the Great Depression and World War II when funds were scarce but his parents worked daily to provide everything needed to sustain their household.

As Randolph took the name of Reverend Boniface Hardin, Order of Saint Benedict, he still remained in touch with his parents. We remember how, periodically, the family would travel the narrow two-lane highway to Saint Meinrad Archabbey with friends to observe his progress, and where prayer, academic achievement, and hard work were strictly observed and required of everyone. The portrait of this experience in the following pages helps to illuminate how this seminary experience unfolded for one of the first students of color at Saint Meinrad.

Following his ordination, Boniface—as we then called him—was still loving but had become more circumspect about his obligations to both his church family and his biological family. We understood that he had moved from being just a sibling: he had become a servant of God in the Roman Catholic Church and the rules of his religious Order of Saint Benedict. Somewhere along the line, we were still there in his heart.

By the end of the 1970s, both of our parents had passed away. Boniface, as the eldest remaining member of this wing of the Hardin family, was now a family leader. Yet, we knew he had adopted another family—the Indianapolis community. Each of us continued to talk with him via phone or visits to Indianapolis. By this same point, each of his brothers had married—Bill married Rebecca White, Albert married Gwendolyn Smith, and John married Maxine Randle. Boniface performed John's wedding at Holy Angels Church in Indianapolis during a December 1973 snowstorm.

When Boniface and Sister Jane Schilling struck out to create Martin Center College (present-day Martin University), he continued the family tradition of teaching started by our schoolteacher parents. Each of us as brothers had limited and distant impact on this period of his life. John contributed articles to the *Afro-American Journal* published by Martin Center College. As an articulate leader among African American Catholics in the Louisville Archdiocese, Bill provided a practical laymen's counsel when needed. Bill was not a resident of Indianapolis but he knew what was *right and necessary* within the Roman Catholic Church. Albert became an active leader in his Louisville parish and often had conversations with his "big" brother. Lastly, John, the youngest of the four and a college-level teacher, got to know Boniface more clearly in the latter years of his life during lengthy phone calls discussing a wide array of issues, including higher education.

Overall, as his three brothers, we recognized that as Randolph became Boniface, he evolved as did we. All of us developed our own families, experienced pleasant days, sufferings with the loss of loved ones, and faced personal physical challenges. The immediate Boniface Hardin family was not biological per se but had other members in Saint Meinrad and Indianapolis.

The following chapters will expand your knowledge of Boniface's Kentucky roots and his Saint Meinrad and Indianapolis years. The author of these chapters is Dr. Nancy Chism, an Indianapolis resident and collegiate academic

The Hardin family in 1969. **Front:** *Boniface, John, Elizabeth, and Albert A.* **Back:** *Albert T., and Bill.*

administrator familiar with many of the events, movements, and challenges Boniface faced during most of his years in the city. Using her personal recollections combined with archival documents from the Indiana Historical Society, a key interview from the Indiana University Oral History Project, his personal papers from Martin University, and immediate family interviews, Doctor Chism has crafted a sensitive, nuanced understanding of how Randolph Hardin from Kentucky became Reverend Boniface Hardin, OSB, as well as an educator for all Indianapolis communities regardless of race, creed, or personal status.

Finally, we are convinced that Boniface believed that all life is a gift from God, and living well the life given to us is a test to see if we were worthwhile recipients. We hope that the story of Boniface's life in these pages will inspire others to follow in his footsteps and pass their own test.

William A. Hardin Sr.
Albert T. Hardin
John A. Hardin
August 2017

Preface

The room was like many rehabilitation-center rooms—painted in a muted color and furnished in Spartan décor—set within a background of calling voices, rubberized shoes pounding along the halls, and the metallic clang of gurneys and equipment carts outside the door. Father Boniface Hardin sat quietly, reflecting on the stroke he had suffered and thinking about his future. The left side of his body had been affected, rendering it difficult for him to control his facial movements or use his arm. He knitted his brow and said, "One thing I regret is that I never got the story down." "The story of your life and work?" I asked. He nodded. "I've wanted to do it for a long time. I just ran out of time." I was touched by his sorrow, swallowed hard, and said, "I can do that for you."

Father Hardin intended to call his biography, "Pickin' Cotton on the Way to Church." Undoubtedly, this title was to refer to his experience as an African American Catholic. His family's roots in slavery and his experience in the Catholic Church, including having to sit in the back corner of the church, having to receive Communion last, being barred from entering the seminary, and experiencing disciplinary action for his social-justice efforts, all contributed to his troubled relationship with the institutional Church. Although cotton was not cultivated in his native Kentucky, the classic work of slaves was Father's metaphor for the ways in which he continually had to earn his right to be Catholic. I have used his title for this work to honor his intentions and insights.

To me, Father Hardin was priest and colleague. As a Catholic, I attended masses he offered and looked forward to his homilies. He was an endearingly folksy speaker, humble, prone to wander, but compelling. His remarks were deeply meaningful to me, and the messenger who delivered them seemed especially authentic and lovable. As a colleague, Father came to talk to my classes on the culture of higher education at the Indiana University School of Education in Indianapolis. I asked him to talk about what he and Sister Jane Schilling had created at Martin University. He demonstrated, rather than addressed this topic with words, by taking the better part of his speaking time to go from one student to another, holding them in his gaze and asking them what their goals were, who they were.

When I offered to write Father's story, I did not know how little information would be available to complete the task. It was clear that Father himself could not participate in any lengthy conversations, but I assumed that there were good records of this man who had become a public figure, a larger-than-life person in the Indianapolis community. I was wrong. Father spoke from the heart, not from printed scripts. He had no archivists or scholarly experts to maintain and preserve the printed documents associated with his life. Following his death, his close associates were required to throw his belongings into boxes and hastily transport them from his cluttered home to various interim storage places. They were in no particular order and the contents of many boxes were damaged by water and mice. Many documents at Martin University pertinent to Father's work had been discarded or haphazardly stored by his immediate successor.

I began to try to sort what materials existed, comb newspapers and websites for information about Father Hardin, and look for any archival materials preserved in libraries. I soon realized, however, that I had to talk with people to supplement the sparse paper trail. At the heart of the work presented here are the testimonies of more than forty people who generously gave of their time to contribute oral-history interviews. They endowed me with a rich store of memories, commentaries, and insights that turned the business of research into a warm and touching experience. As I transcribed their words and listened to their laughter, witnessed their struggles to fight back tears, and felt the love that they had for Father Hardin, I was inspired as well as informed. Quotations from these oral histories abound in the document; they are more apt renderings than I, or perhaps any scholar, would be able to provide.

At regular points in this project, I have questioned my rashness in volunteering to write this story. Before undertaking this project, I had never worked closely with Father Hardin or Martin University, and I am not a member of the African American community in Indianapolis. I did not live in Indianapolis for much of Father's history in this city. Yet I experienced him as a person and felt his warmth. I deeply admired his vision and commitment. Although not a historian, I have a scholarly background, and, most of all, I was there when he worried about the preservation of his history. I was the answer to the call. I hope that my efforts, both in what I have written in this book, and in my attempts to build an archive at the Indiana Historical Society William Henry Smith Memorial Library, for future scholars, will keep the legacy of this phenomenal man alive.

Acknowledgments

As I contemplate thanking those who helped in the preparation of this book, I am smiling. First of all, I am recollecting the look of relief and loving gratitude on the face of Father Boniface Hardin when I said I would undertake this project. He is the source of inspiration, the loving presence who inspired me from the start and continued to bless this project from his place in the world that surrounds us.

I smile too in remembering all of the wonderful conversations I had with those who knew Father Hardin. Each time I conducted one of the more than forty interviews for this project, I set out to meet a stranger, but returned with a new friend. As interviewer and participants, we shared a love and respect for Father Hardin: this bond situated the conversations within an atmosphere of respect, fondness, and loyalty. I often found that as interviews progressed, laughter and tears mingled with struggles to remember and describe fully the experience of having known Father Hardin. I am moved by the generosity of those I interviewed in making time for me to talk with them, record their words, and give permission for these small oral histories to be added to the Father Boniface Hardin Collection established at the Indiana Historical Society William Henry Smith Memorial Library. The names of these wonderful people are in the appendix to this biography. Without their help, I would not have been able to tell the story.

Stefanie Lee, who unselfishly took care of Father Hardin during his illness and also cared for Sister Jane Schilling, his closest associate, has been a crucial partner in the writing of this story. Having struggled to collect and preserve Father Hardin's belongings after his death, Stefanie and Greg Johnson fought off several attempts to dispose of important records and possessions. Her gift of those records and photographs constitutes the major part of the IHS's Father Boniface Hardin Collection. Due to her vigilance and loyalty, there is a record that other scholars can use in the future to do research on this remarkable man. As a supportive friend throughout the process of writing the biography, Stefanie not only helped to make connections with potential interviewees but also filled in gaps in the information with her own recollections.

Professor Andrea Walton, my colleague at Indiana University, showed deep interest in the project from the start. As an historian, she mentored me in the conventions of biographical writing. More importantly, she became enthusiastic about the need to tell the story of Father Boniface. She helped by checking interview transcripts, reading and commenting on drafts, and suggesting solutions to my many questions. Andrea also initiated two collaborative scholarly projects on Father Boniface's life—conference presentations and publication of a scholarly essay. Her help has been invaluable and her friendship, another gift that has come my way.

Father Hardin's brothers have also been essential contributors to this project. His youngest brother, Professor John Hardin, is the second historian who helped me navigate the ways in which life stories are told. He has read and critiqued drafts, helped with family history questions, and provided important contextual documents and information. Oldest brother Bill Hardin, closest in age to Father Hardin, was able to draw on a phenomenal memory to create marvelously colorful depictions of incidents in the life of his older brother as he grew up. Middle brother Albert helped with his own memories and added details. All three brothers collaborated on the foreword, for which I am grateful.

The family of Sister Jane Shilling also provided invaluable information. Sisters Fern (Snooks) Wenger and Jane Jelinski both contributed details about Sister Jane's life and as Father Hardin's "second family," they also supplied information about Father Hardin, who relied on them for the kind of support that only extended family can supply. In addition, Snooks Wenger provided photographs of the young Sister Jane and warm and enthusiastic enouragement throughout the writing process.

Father Bruce Knox, former colleague of Father Hardin and teacher at Martin University, helped a great deal with transcription and interview checking. The late Wilma Moore from the Indiana Historical Society contributed her time and expertise in helping to initiate the Father Boniface Hardin Collection. Jennifer McCloud, Lydia Morton, and President Emeritus Eugene White at Martin University were extremely generous with their time and permission to access and use materials at Martin University. White also read a draft and generously provided the afterword. Archabbot Justin Duvall, Father Vincent Tobin, Mary Jeanne Schumaker, and Krista Hall from Saint Meinrad Archabbey also helped with important details, photos, and permissions.

Family and friends were the backbone of my support system. Mary Breckenridge read and commented on a draft. Others consistently cheered me on and reinforced the importance of telling Father Hardin's story. My daughters, Angela, Lauren, and Elizabeth, never wavered in their confidence in me. Above all, my husband Grady not only tolerated, but also encouraged the expenditure of time and resources I devoted to this project. He and Boniface had a special connection. Because Father Hardin often said, "Can I get an 'Amen' to that?" Grady made a stained-glass AMEN for the fiftieth anniversary of Father's ordination. In like manner, Grady has also given a resounding "Amen" to this project, without which it would not be possible. For these and others too numerous to mention, I am eternally grateful.

Chapter 1

THE EARLY YEARS, 1933–65: FROM YOUNG RANDY
TO FATHER BONIFACE HARDIN, OSB

"My life [as a child] was the church and the community." [1]

The days leading up to Boniface Hardin's birth on November 18, 1933, were likely a time of great anxiety for his parents, Albert Augustine and Elizabeth Hansbro Hardin. Only eighteen months earlier, their first-born son, Albert Arthur, died shortly after birth. This time, as labor began, the young couple traveled to Louisville General Hospital, where black people who did not have healthcare in the rural regions were served.[2] To his parents' great relief, their child, named James Dwight Randolph Hardin, was healthy and lively. Family and friends began to call him "Randy,"[3] highlighting his third name, which was inspired by A. Philip Randolph, the founder of the Brotherhood of Sleeping Car Porters. Randolph was a frequent visitor to the home of Randy's maternal grandfather, Arthur Hansbro, a train porter who was proud of his work and later regaled his grandchildren with his uniform and stories of far-away places.

Slavery was still a presence in the history of Kentucky and in the story of Randy's origins. His great-grandfather, believed by some in the family to be the slave of an owner called Briggs, was adopted as an orphan by a woman named Hardin, who gave him her name.[4] The area in which the Hardin family lived centered on Bardstown, adjacent to Hardin County, which was named after a lawyer, Benjamin Hardin, who had emigrated from France. It is said that Randy's grandfather, Will, and his father, Albert, who both had light complexions and could have passed for white, resembled the men in Benjamin Hardin's family but no firm link has been established.[5] Elizabeth's family home was in Elizabethtown and she was partly of Indian ancestry on her mother, Mollie Crowe's, side.

The area around Bardstown was settled during the eighteenth century mainly by families who moved west from Maryland in search of fertile land. Because Baltimore, Maryland, was the seat of the first Catholic diocese in the United States, the majority of the settlers were Catholic. As the migration into Kentucky continued, Bardstown was chosen in 1808 as the seat of one of the

Clockwise from top left: Elizabeth Hansbro as a college student, between 1925 and 1929; Randy and brother Bill, about 1940; Grandfather Arthur Hansbro; Father (Albert A. Hardin), young Randy, and mother (Elizabeth Hansbro Hardin) about 1934.

first four Catholic dioceses in the country, with extensive boundaries stretching from the Gulf of Mexico to Canada and the Appalachian Mountains to the Mississippi River.[6] The settlers from the East brought slaves and established a system of importing, owning, and trading slaves that lasted until the ratification of the Thirteenth Amendment legally ended slavery. Traditionally, those who were Catholic baptized their slaves into the Catholic religion.[7] Bardstown

Randy Hardin, left rear, brother Bill Hardin, right front, and cousins, early 1940s.

Saint Joseph Protocathedral in Bardstown, Kentucky. Hardin slave ancestors were conscripted in its construction.

became the site of Saint Joseph, the fifth Catholic cathedral in the United States, an edifice that was built in part by slave labor, including slaves from the Hardin family. Slavery was pervasive in the Catholic Church; nuns who wished to enter the Nazareth Motherhouse in Bardstown were required to bring a slave as their dowry.[8]

The Hardin family believed that their Catholic origins came through Randy's paternal grandmother, Louise Settles Hardin. At the time, Catholic couples with religious "mixed marriages" had to pledge to raise their children Catholic. Although Louise's husband, Will, was Methodist, his children, including Randy's father, Albert, were raised Catholic. Will was a waiter at the Old Talbott Tavern in Bardstown and was mentioned in *Ripley's Believe It or Not* for never having missed a day of work in fifty years. He became somewhat of a legend in his day; townsfolk said that one could set the clocks by the moment of his arrival at work.[9] When Albert married Elizabeth Hansbro, who was raised Baptist, she pledged to raise the children Catholic. Elizabeth converted to Catholicism when her son, Randy, was eleven years old.

The Hardins were highly educated for the time, having both graduated in 1929 from normal school at Kentucky State Industrial College for Colored Persons, which eventually became Kentucky State University. Over time, Albert and Elizabeth had three more sons: William, Albert Thomas, and John. Their one daughter, Elizabeth Ann, as well as their firstborn son, Albert Arthur, died at birth. For the first four years of Randy's life, his parents taught in New Haven, Kentucky, schools for colored children. Since teaching did not pay well, Albert at first supplemented his position by opening a restaurant and small grocery store. After a brief move to Fairfield, Kentucky, where there were no teaching jobs, the family moved to Bardstown, but Elizabeth continued to travel to New Haven to teach. In Bardstown Albert followed in the footsteps of his father and became a waiter, a job that paid a higher salary than teaching. He continued to operate a small grocery store out of the family's duplex on Brashear Street, working at the store during the day and as a waiter at night.[10]

During Randy's days in Bardstown, life in the Hardin family was happy and calm. William (Bill) Hardin, his younger brother by four years, recalled that the family "had all the natural things that kids had," including a car and a dog named Scottie. Their rural home had an outhouse, an outdoor water faucet, and a wood-burning stove. The Hardin boys had chores connected with such tasks as hauling wood to the house and were disciplined quickly for any slacking. Their parents were strict but loving and continually stressed education for

their children.[11] Albert was known as a proud man, an avid reader, and someone who expected obedience from his family, loved them fiercely, and strived
to support them.[12] Elizabeth was known for her intelligence, her loyalty to her
profession and students, and her nurturing attention to her sons. She and
Randy had an especially close bond throughout their lives. Randy later recalled
that his family life was very routine and ordered: "There was recreation—you
know, parks and things—but as far as I was concerned I flew back home [from
school] and did my chores after work and then got my homework and then on
Saturdays and Sundays you know maybe we went to visit relatives or some-

*Elizabeth and Albert with eleven-year-old altar boy, Randy, on the day of his mother's First
Holy Communion, 1945. The priest in background is Father Simon Griesam of Saint Peter
Claver Church in Louisville, Kentucky.*

thing like that, but I sat out on the porch and we went to church on Sunday and come back and . . . I served mass, so I had to get up at 6 o'clock in the morning and 7:30 in the summertime. And that was for some of us like a community and it wasn't that way for everybody, but my father and mother . . . we led a very limited life. We didn't do lots of things, you know, we did a lot of things with ourselves."[13]

The family lived in Saint Joseph Parish, which by this time was no longer the center of the diocese, since Louisville had been named an archdiocese in 1849. The cathedral was now called a protocathedral in deference to the new cathedral in Louisville. Saint Joseph was designated a basilica in 2001.[14] The Hardin family was allowed to attend Mass at the protocathedral but all blacks were relegated to sit in the "Amen corner," an area at the back of the church. "When I was a young person," Randy later recalled, "we used to have to sit in the back of the church, you know, in the Catholic church. I used to have to sit in the back. There was a sign that said 'Colored.' And we used to get real mad because we had our little section in the back of the church and then when the white folks would come they would push us out of our seats. And we'd get really mad because when they came and took our seats, we didn't have any place to go and we didn't dare move out of our territory."[15]

Young Randy was permitted to make his first Holy Communion in the church, but had to wait until all the white children had received Communion. Shortly after, the pastor, Father Michael Lally, initiated a move to build a separate church for black Catholics, a move opposed by Albert, who pointed out that one of his great-grandfathers, a blacksmith slave, had helped build the cathedral. Albert protested that the Hardin family should have the same rights to continue to attend as any other parishioner. As Bill recounted, "He said, 'This is our church. We put the church together.' We were a part of the church family, even though we had to move to the left and to the rear, [taking the sacrament] after other folks had."[16] Nevertheless, a new church, Saint Monica, was established for black parishioners.[17]

At first, Mass for the black Catholics in the area was held in Saint Monica School, where black children were educated. Although Saint Joseph had a Catholic school, the Day Law of 1904 in Kentucky mandated segregation in education, affecting the schooling of young Randy and his brothers. Early on, Randy became entranced with Catholic ritual and became an altar boy. His affinity for languages surfaced during this period; he could recite all the Latin prayers that were used in the Catholic Church before the Second Vatican Council reforms

Saint Peter Claver Church, Louisville, Kentucky

allowed the Mass to be said in the local language.[18] Bill recalled that Randy was serious: "He didn't like to do the boy things that I liked to do like throw rocks, climb trees, and scuffle and get in fights and stuff like that."[19]

Bill later wrote a short play depicting an incident that illustrated Randy's early piety. At the height of the polio epidemic, when the Hardins informed their sons that they had to stay home from church one Sunday to avoid being exposed, Bill was ecstatic, thinking he could play while his parents went to the Mass. He was in the care of his serious older brother, however, and Randy demanded that Bill kneel for a "mass" that Randy offered in strict imitation of those he regularly attended.[20]

As the World War II need for manpower ramped up, Albert was given some choices in the draft. Since he was a father and necessary to the support of his family, he was offered the option of working in the defense industry. His new employment was at the Jeffersonville Boatworks, a company in southern Indiana that made landing craft and other military water equipment. Reluctantly, the family had to relocate to nearby Louisville, where they lived in an area called Smoketown with other black residents. Smoketown (said to be named for the many brick manufacturing kilns or flour mills that were located in the area in the early nineteenth century)[21] was a place carved out for black people who served white people as housemaids, factory workers, or other laborers in greater Louisville. Elizabeth continued to teach at the school in New Haven, ensuring that black children there had access to education, journeying sixty-five miles back and forth by car, and finally by rail when the car failed.[22]

The Hardin family lived a block away from a Catholic church and school that served black families, Saint Peter Claver. It was staffed by Franciscan priests and had been founded by Mother Katharine Drexel, who served the Indian and "Negro" missions. The pastor of the church, a German priest named Father Simon Griesam, was devoted to his parishioners and formed a drum-and-bugle corps that played at weddings, festivals, and parades. Randy played the trumpet and xylophone. Griesam was adamant that the Saint Peter Claver corps not be placed last in parades, the usual position for black bands, but rather march up front or in the middle with the white bands.[23] Griesam walked with the corps, straw hat in hand. "We were his pride and joy but we were proud of him, too, erect and always in step," Randy recalled.[24]

Ursuline sisters staffed Saint Peter Claver School, which had few resources. The school worked with nearby white Catholic communities in the German-town and Paristown sections of Louisville to supplement its materials. Being

Classroom at Saint Peter Claver School, mid-1940s. Randy Hardin is the tall student in the back.

HARDIN FAMILY COLLECTION

a tall, smart, and conscientious student, Randy was often selected for errands and was regularly sent to push a large cart along the city streets to pick up used books and materials from the white schools. Although the books were marked and had pages missing, the children at Saint Peter Claver were happy to get them.[25]

Later in life, Father Hardin reflected on the difficulties involved in being black and also a Catholic. He recalled that his family did not worry about that much, but some internal friction arose between his mother's Baptist family and his father's Catholic family traditions, especially when his mother converted and was considered to be a "traitor." Father Hardin remembered with amusement how his non-Catholic playmates were very wary of the Catholic Church: "They'd hold their hand over their mouth afraid that their teeth would fall out if they see two nuns walking down the street, you know, and if they said anything when they walked by them [they believed] they'd grow a tail."[26]

As an adult reflecting back on black-white relations in his youth, Father Hardin said that in a context where lynchings were still taking place, he was taught not to mingle with white folks, to keep his eyes down when in their company, and to avoid altercations with them at all times.[27] Speaking about himself, he said, "He was the colored boy who had to sit in the balcony at Saturday matinees in Bardstown and had to step behind the white line when he rode the bus in Louisville. He was the boy who read about lynchings in the *Colored Defender* newspaper [the present-day *Louisville Defender*] but never heard such subjects discussed at home, because they were 'too painful.'"[28]

At school Randy became known as an exceptionally smart student and was sent to workshops and conferences in the neighboring Catholic communities. He was known for his devotion to the Church and routinely served as an altar boy at the 6:30 a.m. masses. Griesam, and the school principal, Sister Inez Stauble, were impressed with Randy's grasp of Latin and his school performance in general. When Randy told them that he felt he had a calling to be a priest, they were very supportive, as was Father Michael Lally from his previous school, Saint Monica in Bardstown.[29] The priests spoke to the Hardin family about the vocation and urged them to support Randy's calling.

When Randy approached his eighth-grade graduation at the age of thirteen, he decided that he would enter the seminary. At the time, many young aspirants to the priesthood entered a seminary high school with the intention of staying through several stages of education until they were ordained. Things were not so simple, however, for a young black boy. He encountered resistance from the initial seminaries he sought to enter. The Catholic Church interpreted that the Day Law, which prohibited integrated schooling, applied to seminaries. Randy, therefore, was not welcome to enter the Louisville seminary. The young boy was deeply disappointed. Undaunted, his proponents made a strong effort to find a seminary that would accept black novices.[30]

In 1920 the Society of Divine Word priests had established Saint Augustine Seminary in Bay-Saint Louis, Mississippi, expressly for black men who wished to become priests. Founding rector Father Matthew Christmann was a pioneer imploring the Catholic Church to welcome the formation of black priests, saying, "It must be clear to everyone that it is surely a grave injustice to exclude a whole race from the priesthood, principally because prejudice will greatly hamper them in their religious activities, or a cordial cooperation with white priests may meet with great obstacles. Such an injustice is bound to work havoc and bring down heavy vengeance upon him who becomes guilty of it."[31]

In spite of the potential welcome in Mississippi, the Hardin family was strongly opposed to sending Randy so far away and also did not have the funds for transportation and other expenses, so the search continued. Albert and Griesam approached Archbishop John A. Floersh of the Louisville Archdiocese, who had already refused to allow Randy to enter the Louisville seminary, asking about a seminary in southern Indiana, Saint Meinrad, which was beginning an effort to integrate its high school. The archbishop did not welcome the suggestion and refused to support Randy's ambition to become a priest. Since the usual custom in the Catholic Church was for the archbishop to pay for the education of seminarians who would later serve in his diocese, this refusal by the archbishop presented an enormous challenge to Randy's aspirations and the Hardin family budget.[32] Without the archbishop's support, Randy's prospects for the priesthood looked extremely bleak.

The black community of Saint Peter Claver and Randy's family members and friends were heartbroken but they were bound and determined to find a way for him to go to Saint Meinrad. Bill recalled that the people in the parish said, "We're gonna help Mrs. Hardin out because he's our son too. . . . So they got it together, they did fish fries, they did chittlin' dinners, they did suppers, they raised money and without question sent it off."[33] They bargained with the vendors of the supplies Randy was supposed to have in order to get cheaper prices. They helped the Hardin family economize by sewing the cassocks and other clothing a young seminarian needed, rather than purchasing them ready-made. In contrast to the other students who were being financially supported by their bishops, there was a full-press grassroots effort behind Randy as he entered the seminary.[34]

Although the Hardin family dreaded life without Randy, they felt enormous pride in their son's vocation. "They were taller, they were everything," Bill recalled. "Every time in church, the people, the respect they got [was uplifting]."[35] With two sons at home—William, eight, and Albert, one—and a third son, John, to be born two years later, the family was in the midst of child rearing while Randy completed his high school years one state away. Albert Sr. had moved from his wartime employment with the Jeffersonville Boatworks to a position with the Louisville and Nashville Railroad, where he worked until his retirement.

Saint Meinrad Archabbey had been established in 1854 by monks from the Einsiedeln Abbey in Switzerland who had been asked to come to Indiana to serve the growing German immigrant population and help prepare priests for them. The monks in the abbey live according to the rule of Saint Benedict, who wrote guidelines for religious living in community in the sixth century. The monks ordained at Saint Meinrad, called Benedictines, pray together five times a day. Most monks are scholars and teachers; some do parish work, and others choose to engage in arts and crafts within the monastery.[36] During Randy's attendance, the minor seminary consisted of four years of high school and two years of liberal arts. The major seminary consisted of two years of philosophy and four years of theology.

Freshman class of 1945–46 at Saint Meinrad Seminary. Randy (Father Hardin) is the middle student in the back row.

Until just before Randy's entrance, Saint Meinrad Seminary educated only white candidates for the priesthood. Under Archabbot Ignatius Esser, the monastery was opened to black students and seminarians. The presence of Archbishop (later Cardinal of Saint Louis) Joseph Ritter in Indianapolis, who was a champion of social justice and equality, was likely a supportive factor.[37] The first black seminarian to become a monk at Saint Meinrad, Father Cyprian Davis, remembered that the influx of funds from the GI Bill enabled some black men to afford private college education and it was thus in the interest of Saint Meinrad to attract these students. Davis, who initially studied at Catholic University in Washington, DC, came to Saint Meinrad for seminary study, professed his vows as a monk in 1951, and was ordained in 1956, three years before Randy. A pioneer himself, Father Cyprian recalls that black minstrel shows were only discontinued at the seminary in 1950, five years after Randy became a student.[38]

Randy's studies during high school followed a classical curriculum. He focused on Greek, Latin, and German, as well as the other liberal arts and sciences. Students had twenty-five hours of classes, twenty-plus hours of study, twenty hours of prayer, and a few hours of recreation each week. Although Randy was known as a top student in Louisville, Davis remembered him as an average student, given the context of very high expectations for scholarship at Saint Meinrad.[39] Later, Randy recalled feeling that there were low expectations for his success: "When we came up, you had to be super good, just to get entrance, you had to [have] all kinds of qualifications. And all along the way, there was constant scrutiny, I mean, not just whether you knelt up straight or whether you looked right, your clothes were clean, everything. I mean they scrutinized you inside and out."[40] Father Bob Kolentus, a former classmate, said that Randy was nicknamed "Bones," perhaps because he was tall and thin. He was known as a friendly and laid-back student.[41] Father Vincent Tobin, another classmate, speculated that Randy was called "Bones" because he played bongo drums in a school play with his fingers, which made the sounds of bones striking the drums.[42]

Following high school, Randy was admitted to the seminary. Three other black students entered the Saint Meinrad seminary at the same time. Two, Jessie Cotton and Charles Edward Payne (Randy's cousin) were from Bardstown, and another, John Howard, was from Saint Peter Claver Church in Louisville. Two of these intended to become brothers, which at the time required the least amount of training, and the other one hoped to become a diocesan priest. At Saint Meinrad, the most difficult path to follow was preparation to be a monk, which required an extra year of study beyond that required for diocesan priests. This was the path that Randy longed to follow. He later remembered how the black students tried to become mainstream, resulting in isolation: "We made a special effort to stay away from each other because we didn't want to be segregated. That was the one thing all our parents told us to be sure and don't be off to yourself. And we went to the other extreme."[43] By the end of the first year, he was the only one of the four black students who persisted at Saint Meinrad.[44] The strange environment and culture, along with racism within the Church and lack of support for these new students, were insurmountable obstacles for all but the determined Randy.

As he studied in a mostly white environment, Randy was called upon to reconsider his racial identity. "The whole question regarding race and so forth had just begun. And it's then that that affected him," noted Davis. "He began to be much more open to what was happening in terms of race. I was talking about it, he was talking about it, some of the students were and so forth."[45] Davis recalled that Randy began to take an interest in Martin Luther King Jr. and the early events connected with the Civil Rights Movement as his studies progressed. During the years prior to his ordination, dramatic events had occurred, including the 1954 *Brown vs. Board of Education* Supreme Court decision on school desegregation; the killing of Emmitt Till; the refusal of Rosa Parks to sit in the back of the bus and the ensuing boycott in Montgomery, Alabama; the passage of the Civil Rights Act of 1957; and the establishment of the Southern Christian Leadership Conference by King and Ralph Abernathy. As both men studied, they were often reminded that the idea of racial equality was quite new to many of their classmates. Interestingly, two of his white classmates do not recall issues of race coming up with Randy; perhaps discussion was quite muted.[46]

Randy's professors might have been learning about racial prejudice themselves. In a folder of his term papers done between 1954 and 1959, Randy included two book reviews, one of the *Dred Scott Case* by Vincent Hopkins, SJ, and the other, a review of Russel Nye's *Fettered Freedom*, which is about slavery and abolition. In the latter review, Randy wrote, "I felt when I had finished the book that I wanted to fight slavery and its effects with all the strength in me."[47] Interestingly, the paper was graded a "C" with no comments. In talking later in life about his taking part in an Abraham Lincoln contest as a deacon, he recalled that as he delivered Lincoln's Jonesboro speech, he was torn in his opinion of Lincoln, who supported repatriation of slaves to Africa.[48] Tobin,

Father Boniface Hardin as a new monk at Saint Meinrad Archabbey, between 1956 and 1959.

Boniface Hardin and seminarian John Caskey became deacons before ordination, May 1958.

who recalled Randy as "very amiable," stated that conformity is stressed during seminary days, and that Randy kept a low profile like the others in his class.[49]

Randy's family came often to see him during his stay at Saint Meinrad. The seminarians became used to seeing members of the extended Hardin family coming to support Randy when visits were permitted.[50] Bill remembered one positive story of support. When Randy was traveling back to Louisville for a program with a few of his classmates, the group got off the bus at a segregated station and stopped for something to eat. The waitress asked Randy if he was "colored," and when he replied that he was, she declined to serve him. His classmates stood up and told the waitress that in that case, they would not eat there either.[51]

Randy also found some support in seminary policies that were less racially restrictive than those in Kentucky, such as being allowed to choose where to sit in church. Looking back, he talked about how he, as a seminarian, had to navigate both worlds: "Even when I was a student in the ministry, I still had to sit in the back, in Kentucky, I had to sit in the back of the church. In the second and third year of high school, I was still sitting in the back of the church. Now when I went across the Ohio River and got into Indiana . . . I sat up front, I sat all the way up front, you know. Most people like to sit in the back, but I sat all the way in the front of the church."[52]

In order to help finance his education, Randy had to work on holidays and summers during high school. He found work at the Ursuline Motherhouse in Louisville, where they had a farm. The job involved such farm work as planting, plowing, and harvesting, which might explain the title of his planned (but never executed) autobiography, "Pickin' Cotton on the Way to Church." Bill related an incident that he regarded as a true test of Randy's character. One summer when Bill developed a ruptured appendix and contracted peritonitis, his father could not afford the new medicine that was prescribed, so Randy provided the seven dollars needed for each dose needed to keep his brother alive from his education fund. In so doing, he gave up a day's wages for each dose, jeopardizing his tuition resources. Randy had to take on extra work to save enough money to get through the term.[53]

As Randy reached the end of his minor seminary days, he made the formal commitment to become a monk. Men who made this decision stepped out of the regular seminarian education sequence to spend a year learning the Rule of Saint Benedict and practicing its prescriptions. He chose this path in the face of perceived resistance: "I always just kind of felt like they [his superiors] would say, 'Well, you should be a brother, you can't be a priest.' And I was doing very well. But there was always that feeling I was expected to fail. . . . It was communicated to me through my teachers, and it was communicated to me by means of the people who lived around me."[54] Randy had been at Saint Meinrad for six years. With his first vows in 1953, he received the name of Boniface.

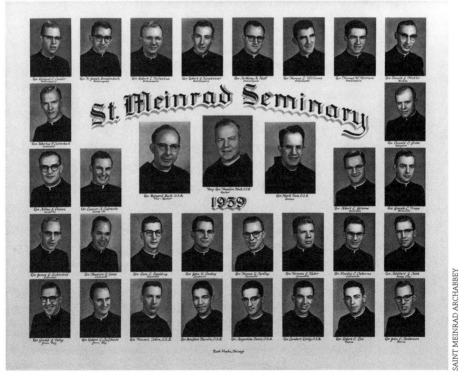

Saint Meinrad Archabbey Ordination class, 1959. Father Hardin is fourth from left, bottom row.

SAINT MEINRAD ARCHABBEY

The name Boniface means "doer of good," and throughout his life Father Hardin was proud to carry the name. He regarded Boniface as a "tough guy" who chopped down the pagan oak to bring Catholicism to Germany.[55]

The reasons for Randy's decision to become both a monk and a priest are not explained in any of his later remarks. It is not known whether he was encouraged by one of his teachers or religious figures in his life. From his subsequent talks, teaching, and conversation, however, it is clear that he loved Latin and Greek, philosophy, and theology. Since monks who were also priests were thought to be the most intellectual of the priests at the abbey, it might be that Randy sought to pursue a life of scholarship. At any rate, the decision to become a monk is usually something that is made gradually, as one studies and reflects.[56] Randy most likely had been thinking about becoming a monk for some time.

After studying philosophy and theology for four more years, Father Hardin made his solemn vows in 1957, ten years after he began his studies at Saint Meinrad. On May 11, 1959, a day that he described as "the most important day of my life,"[57] he was ordained into the priesthood. During the final formation period from 1953 to 1959 he was not allowed to leave the monastery to visit his family in Louisville, a custom that was in line with the practices of

SAINT MEINRAD ARCHABBEY

First Mass for Father Boniface (center), 1959.

monastic preparation at the time. At the end of this period, his family came to Saint Meinrad, not only to celebrate his ordination, but also to rejoice in being able to have him back in close contact.

At Father Hardin's First Mass, celebrated in the Saint Meinrad College chapel, he was assisted by Fathers Brien and Daniel Buechlein (later to be his archbishop) and Michael Langston. Hardin's mother and Mary Scott Crowe attended. In the summary of the day, he wrote about the breakfast that followed: "I tried to get the servers to eat with us, but I didn't succeed. I used Fr. Bede's vestment (with the daggers)."[58] A press release about the event listed Father Hardin as the "first negro to be ordained a priest from the city of Louisville and the second negro from Kentucky."[59]

The new Father Hardin said one of his first masses in Louisville, with his proud family and community members in attendance. He was also invited to serve as deacon at the dedication of Saint Rita Church in Indianapolis. The pastor, Father Bernard Strange, wrote to Father Hardin's superior, Archabbott Bonaventure Knabel, saying, "Since 99% of St. Rita's membership is Negro, I feel that I owe it to the members to have at least one Negro priest as Deacon or sub-Deacon of the Solemn High Mass."[60] The weeks following Hardin's ordination were filled with a flurry of invited masses and visits to parishes in Indiana.[61]

In the year before his ordination, Father Hardin, as was the custom with all new monks, had been asked what role he wanted to assume as his first placement. Traditionally, the Prefect of Studies would make these decisions following conversations with the students. Many would ask to continue their studies in the United States or abroad; some would ask for an assignment with a parish or within the archabbey. It is not known what preferences Father Hardin expressed. Davis pointed out that Father Hardin was not sent abroad to study or to do a doctorate at some prestigious institution,[62] but was assigned to be assistant treasurer of the archabbey and served in this post for seven years. During this period, he studied accounting at the University of Notre Dame's School of Commerce. Father Hardin might have been disappointed with this assignment, since it was not the path designated for the highest intellectual achievers. He later reflected on how black seminarians fared in their first assignments: "When we came out, we graduated, we weren't put in positions of authority. Now here's a case where your education didn't qualify you for the highest post in that particular order."[63]

Father Hardin described his time as assistant treasurer at the archabbey as a life of working and praying. On many weekends, he responded to invitations from parishes in Indiana to do special programs or to offer Mass. Being naturally an outgoing person, he enjoyed saying Mass and hearing confessions and visiting with parishioners. Those he served continually noticed his status as a black priest, and during many of these visits he encountered surprise that a black person could be a monk and priest. Sometimes he would be asked what country he was from by those who thought he must be African. In one "sundown" city in Indiana, his hosts rushed him out of town, since it would be illegal for him to be out after sunset.[64] In the black parishes of Indianapolis, however, he was viewed with exceptional warmth and fondness. Father Hardin came to enjoy these parish activities much more than his accounting work. He felt that his work as assistant treasurer did not call for him to use any of the special knowledge he gained through his classical education.[65] He also became increasingly invested in the racial-justice discussions and activities taking place in the United States in the early 1960s, when riots burst out in cities and conflicts among the civil rights leaders arose with respect to peaceful or militant approaches. He began to hope for a special call to add purpose to his life. This was to come in 1965.

Chapter 2

THE HOLY ANGELS YEARS, 1965–69: TURMOIL AND A TURNING POINT

*"I was used to getting up at 20 minutes to 4 to start my day with prayers at
4 a.m. I was used to a very structured life. And here, all of a sudden, I was
subject to everyone who came to my door. It was frightening. . . . I was very,
very angry. I was on everybody's case, attacking everybody in government,
poor old Governor [Edgar] Whitcomb and Mayor [Richard] Lugar. But I had
new realizations. It was like a sleeping giant was inside of me, and all of
sudden, he stood up."[1]*

The year 1965 ushered in a new era in Father Boniface Hardin's life—an era that began turbulently and ended with the long period of creativity and leadership that defined his legacy. In June of that year Father Hardin left his post at Saint Meinrad Archabbey to become associate pastor of Holy Angels Parish in Indianapolis, assisting Father Albert Ajamie with parish duties. Two factors appear to have led to this shift: black Catholic priests and laypeople were pushing for greater racial representation among the clergy in Indianapolis parishes, and Father Hardin himself was growing restless with life in the archabbey.

The Catholic Church in Indianapolis had been characterized by a long history of segregation. Black Catholics were served mainly by Saint Bridget Parish downtown and, later, Saint Rita Parish on the east side. Catholic schools were segregated, and Indiana had a very strong tradition of racial animosities. The Ku Klux Klan in Indiana had been extremely strong in the 1920s; an estimated 27 to 40 percent of white males were members.[2] The Klan was particularly strong in central Indiana, where the Indiana General Assembly actually established a KKK day at the Indiana State Fair.[3] Eventually, the Klan was tainted by scandal when Grand Dragon D. C. Stephenson was convicted of the abduction and murder of a young woman.[4] When Stephenson released a list of prominent officials who were accepting funds from the Klan, the group began to decline in popularity. The state's reputation as a hostile environment for blacks, however, continued, despite some positive attributes, such as a flourishing jazz scene on Indianapolis's Indiana Avenue and the absence of large-scale riots during the civil rights era.[5]

Holy Angels Parish was located in northwest Indianapolis, an area of the city that had once been predominately white and middle class. As outmigration to the suburbs occurred and homes were bought for future highway construction, the area became unstable, property values declined, and more black residents moved in.[6] As black Catholics moved into the Holy Angels neighborhood in the 1940s, the question of parish membership became an issue. In an interview for the *Indianapolis News* in 1986 Father Bernard Strange, pastor of Saint Rita Parish, recounted that a previous pastor at Holy Angels, Father James A. Coulter, in 1940 issued a statement of resistance that is still recalled by many Holy Angels parishioners today: "No Negro will ever come to Holy Angels."[7] In other versions of the story, Father Coulter said, "Blacks won't come to Holy Angels as long as I am pastor."[8] Reaction to this statement was so strong that black residents wrote to Pope Pius XII, who is said to have ordered Archbishop (later Cardinal) Joseph Ritter to reassign Father Coulter.[9]

Even with a change in leadership, black Catholics did not experience a warm welcome. Stories told by parishioners more than ten years after Father Coulter's departure illustrate lingering resentment and opposition. One couple, Robert and Ida Treadwell, reported being greeted with "suspicion and caution" when they went to the rectory to inquire about becoming Catholic. Another parishioner, Amanda Strong, recalled that classes for those wishing to convert to Catholicism were segregated.[10]

The integration of Holy Angels School was slow as well. Archbishop Ritter had long been a champion of social justice and in 1938, despite Klan opposition, he ordered an end to segregation of Catholic Schools in Indianapolis. This official pronouncement had not been routinely honored in practice, although four grade schools, in addition to the traditionally black parishes of Saint Rita and Saint Bridget, had a smattering of black students.[11] The public schools were largely the site of de facto segregation and would be involved in a desegregation lawsuit in the 1970s.

Father Boniface Hardin as associate pastor of Holy Angels Catholic Church, Indianapolis, around 1965.

The desegregation of Holy Angels School happened sooner than it did in public schools. Catholic school integration was originally delayed by practices that purportedly were motivated by a desire to avoid overcrowding or underuse of existing schools, as the Archdiocese of Indianapolis manipulated the school assignment plans.[12] By 1949, however, the neighborhood had become so heavily black that the issue could no longer be ignored. Holy Angels School opened that school year with twenty-five black children enrolled.[13] School days for the first of the integrated students were challenging. One of the earliest black students, Joseph Smith, recalled fearful incidents, such as being disciplined for speaking to white female classmates.[14] Alfreda Harvell, the mother of another child, Claudette, was frustrated when a teacher at the school continually questioned why her daughter's hair was "nappy."[15]

The growing presence of black Catholics in the 1950s was not matched by increased numbers of black priests, nationally as well as in Indianapolis. In 1959 Father Hardin was only the eighty-eighth black Catholic priest to be

Hardin distributes Communion with Father Clarence Rivers, Cincinnati, and Father George Clements, Chicago, at the Midwest Clergy Conference on Negro Welfare in October 1960.

INDIANAPOLIS RECORDER COLLECTION, INDIANA HISTORICAL SOCIETY, JIM BURRES ordained in the United States. By 1960 he was one of the 106 black priests among the approximately 50,000 priests in the country. Mynelle Gardner, who later worked with Father Hardin, remembered her surprise at experiencing her first contact with a black priest. As a young girl of ten or eleven, she went to a local Catholic high school to attend a vocation day, a program to encourage young people to consider a life as a priest or nun. She reported that her friends came to her and hollered excitedly, "'You got to see it! You've got to see it!' And I said, 'See what, see what, see what?' They said, 'There's a black priest' And you know, we'd never seen a black priest. They said, 'There's a black priest there.' I said, "Oh, no, there's not . . . you're wrong." And they took me back around to the booth where he [Father Hardin] was, you know, and sure enough, there was a black priest"[16] Charles Blair, also a former Saint Rita student, recalled seeing Father offer a Solemn Mass and having the same incredulous reaction in discovering that the priest was black. He remembered, "It was just inspirational to all the students to see this young, strong, handsome [black] man leading the mass, which we had all held in high esteem, of course, given our religious background. So it was really a pivotal moment for us, for all the students, and for myself, to see this man just kind of leading things, because it had never happened."[17]

Both outright segregation and private discouragement of black entrants within seminaries at the time kept black priests at a minimum, yet as black consciousness and the numbers of black Catholics increased, more and more pressure grew to have black priests as role models and leaders in the Church. In an attempt to serve the growing numbers of black Catholics in the Midwest, the Benedictine community of Saint John Abbey in Collegeville, Minnesota, initiated a priory in South Union, Kentucky, called Saint Maur, intended primarily for the development of black aspirants to the priesthood. The seminary, which later moved to Indianapolis, was led by Father Bernardin Patterson.[18] At the same time, black Catholics were organizing and calling for more voice and representation in the Church. Smith recalled that frequent requests for an increase in black clergy moved Father Patterson and the white pastor of Saint Rita Church, Father Bernard Strange, to recruit Father Hardin for Holy Angels.[19] The priests were especially impressed with Father Hardin, whom they had come to know through his service as visiting priest, a speaker on programs for vocations, and retreats at Saint Rita and other Indianapolis venues. The pastor of Holy Angels, Father Albert Ajamie, pursued the connection with Father Hardin by extending an invitation to him through the Archabbot of Saint Meinrad Archabbey, Bonaventure Knaebel.

As a new priest in June 1960 Hardin (center front) presented a "Women's Day of Reconcili-ation" at Saint Rita Parish. Also pictured, along with the participants, are Father Charles Koster (right) and Father Bernard Strange (left) of Saint Rita.

The invitation to come to Holy Angels was issued at a time when Father Hardin was contemplating his future. As the Civil Rights Movement injected new fervor for social justice and his own personal love of human interaction propelled him, Father Hardin was moved to leave the confines of his post as assistant treasurer of the monastery for an active parish life "Here I had the best education in the world and I'm stuck in a business office," he said in a later interview. "I didn't think it was a good use of my time."[20] He also was feel-ing isolated and separated from his cultural roots. Being in the monastery, he said, "was really a kind of purging, or what do they call it, castration of my own cultural experience. I had no one to talk to. Every time I raised it, everyone'd tell me we had no problems at Saint Meinrad in this area [race relations]."[21] Yet all around him the world was exploding: Malcolm X had come to the forefront, Dr. Martin Luther King had led major protests and had been imprisoned, the March on Washington had occurred, and the Freedom Riders had traveled through the South.

The move to a parish was a somewhat unusual decision for a monk, whose traditional role would be to serve as a scholar and contemplative within the confines of an abbey. Reflecting on the decision, Father Hardin later said, "I think the movement of Dr. King and all that made you more conscious of

Holy Angels Catholic Church, Indianapolis (since demolished).

expending your energies where they could be appreciated. . . . I felt I had a
personal need, my own self-worth. I really had a need at the time to do something that I felt like was contributing to the benefit of the world or my own
people."[22] As he indicated, his decision was likely influenced by the context of
Freedom Summer of 1964, characterized by the passage of the Civil Rights

Act, the creation of the Organization for Afro-American Unity, and the murders of three civil rights workers in Mississippi.

Later in life, Father Hardin recalled his initial intentions in choosing parish life: "I was going to try to do whatever needed to be. If they needed a voice, I'd give them a voice. If they needed somebody to clean, I'd clean." He was conscious that his decision was unusual for a monk and that he would have to make major adjustments. "Monks generally don't go out in parishes and to extraordinary kinds of things," he noted. "So, here I was, in a sense, totally unprepared except for what I learned in theology when they talked to us. So I was really just like a brand new priest. So that's what I did, my attitude, and I trusted people."[23]

His brother, Bill, summarized the family's reaction to Father Hardin's decision to go to Holy Angels: "When we heard that he was going to Indianapolis it was a joy for us because it sort of put us out of this mysterious monastery thing and that he was doing something that we felt deep in our minds and our hearts that he was going to be a priest among the people and a priest among his people." He expressed the sentiment of the time regarding the paucity of black priests: "Because we often knew it was a rarity in those days to see a Negro priest. . . . It was something that was good because it helped the faith, it helped the religion, it helped those people that had concerns about a faith that looked more white than it did as openness to black people. . . . And I think once he got into it he found out what it was all about. And he began to grow."[24]

Several parishioners at Holy Angels recalled Father Hardin's first days. The delight and amazement at seeing a black priest spread like wildfire within the parish. His tall, imposing presence added to the excitement. "My sister, who was in charge of the CYO [Catholic Youth Organization] kids, you know, the kickball teams, back in the day," recalled Joseph Smith, "was there the day Father Boniface pulled up. And she ran home and said, 'There's a colored priest, I saw a colored priest!'"[25]

Father Hardin was to be the second of two assistants at Holy Angels. The plan was for the existing associate, Father Randolph Marshall, to continue his duties while Father Hardin would work specifically in the community and bring more black people into the Catholic Church. However, shortly after he came to Holy Angels, Father Marshall was reassigned and Father Hardin had to assume his responsibilities.[26] Father Hardin's main duties were to say Mass, hear confessions and counsel parishioners, preside at marriages and funerals, help with the management of the parish business, and assist with youth programs.

At first Father Hardin came to these duties with an air of formality. A favorite story told by Sister Jane Schilling, who would become his lifelong associate, centered on an incident that happened when he was touring the

Nancy Schilling, around 1948.

school. Seeing a curse word etched into a desk, Father Hardin angrily said, "This is a disgrace!" On inspecting the desk, Sister Jane countered, "You are so right. They need to learn how to spell these words correctly."[27] Through the tutelage of Sister Jane and others, Father Hardin quickly relaxed into his role and came to appreciate his parishioners.

In Sister Jane, Father Hardin met the person who was to become his most important ally, work associate, and companion in a partnership that lasted until his death. Sister Jane recalled that from the time of their first meeting, "We clicked right away—because we were about the same thing—freedom for African American people."[28]

Born Nancy Schilling in 1930, Sister Jane was the eldest of five children of Lyle Franklin Schilling, a dentist, and his homemaker wife, Rosalie Julia Wolk Schilling, who lived in the northern lake-resort town of Minocqua, Wisconsin. Young Nancy was known for her happy disposition, athleticism, sense of humor, and intelligence. When she learned that the local high school did not provide the preparatory courses she would need to follow in her father's footsteps to become a dentist, she spent her junior and senior years with two aunts in Green Bay, Wisconsin, so that she could take the needed courses at the nearby Saint Joseph Academy. During her high school career, however, she found that she had a vocation to the religious life and began her formation as a Sister of Saint Joseph of Carondelet, whose motherhouse was in Saint Louis, Missouri. She received the name Sister Jane Edward, a combination of her younger sister's and brother's names.[29]

Sister Jane received her bachelor's degree in European and American history at Fontbonne College in Saint Louis and her master's of ancient history at Loyola University in Chicago.[30] A close associate, Stefanie Lee, said that Sister Jane and another sister enjoyed school so much that they continually took courses in areas of interest that would not count toward their degree but would prolong their studies.[31] Sister Jane told her sister, Fern Winger, that she studied ancient history so that she would be assigned to teach older, rather than younger, students.[32]

Sister Jane was first assigned to teach in Saint Rita School in an upper-class Saint Louis neighborhood. While she loved teaching, she really blossomed when she was assigned to Saint Matthew School in an inner-city area where her students were mostly black. Although she confessed that she had only encountered one black person, a railroad worker, in her youth, she quickly became an ardent appreciator of black culture and an advocate for racial equality. While in Saint Louis, Sister Jane was able to help with curriculum development for students at Homer G. Phillips Hospital (for black residents),and to assist in the ministry to ex-convicts at nearby Dismas House, established by Father Frank Zimmerman.

In 1964, when Sister Jane received the "little white card" that the Sisters of Saint Joseph superiors gave the sisters to communicate their next assignments, she was puzzled to discover that she was being sent to Holy Angels Parish in Indianapolis. Her only association with Indianapolis was auto racing[33] but she found upon her arrival that the black, inner-city Holy Angels environment was quite similar to her previous assignment. Sister Jane embraced the opportunity to establish a spirited drum-and-bugle corps, such as the ones she admired in her youth. She and an associate, Sister Pat Quinn, hunted for used instruments and free sheet music for the children.[34]

When Sister Jane was asked to become the principal of Holy Angels School, she used her position to test some of her growing theories about education—the different functioning of the left and right brain, the idea that crawling and psychomotor skill development helped produce success in learning to read, and multiage classroom groupings. She later had a chance to think about applying new theories at the college level as well.[35]

Sister Jane had been at Holy Angels School for a year when Father Hardin arrived on the scene. The two reinforced each other's zeal for social justice and worked in complementary ways for racial understanding and change throughout their forty-seven-year partnership. She was both provocateur to and follower of Father Hardin's ideas as he emerged as an activist black priest.

Amanda Strong, a longtime Holy Angels parishioner, recalled that Father Hardin was "A quick learner. Because it was kind of like his spirit must have been just crouched up, he was waiting for it to just come out of him so he could be himself. It was like he had just to follow all these norms and stuff because he was in that [monastic] community, but once he got out, he could be himself."[36]

The Indianapolis community prior to Father Hardin's arrival had slowly mobilized for the civil rights struggle. After several appearances by King in 1959 and following years, Reverend Andrew J. Brown of Saint John Missionary Baptist Church provided leadership for the establishment of a local chapter of the Southern Christian Leadership Conference. A local chapter of the Congress on Racial Equality was founded in 1964, joining the National Association for the Advancement of Colored People as a third Indianapolis organization advocating peaceful solutions and moderation. As more militant sentiment grew and members of the Black Muslims and other radical groups came to the city, the Indianapolis Urban League was established in 1965 to help bridge the gap.[37]

The Indiana legislature had passed a Civil Rights Law in 1963 that supported equal education and employment and access to such public accommodations as hotels, restaurants, transportation, and theaters, and entrusted enforcement to a Civil Rights Commission. A stronger fight addressing discrimination in housing was fought over the ensuing years. In comparison with other large U.S. cities, the struggle for equal rights in Indianapolis was more subdued. Activists such as Brown attributed this to the overwhelming strength of the white power structure and the lack of motivation on the part of African Americans to take part in the fight, particularly those who had achieved some upward mobility.[38]

Given the context of the civil rights era, Father Hardin's racial consciousness developed rapidly. At that point in his life he had been schooled by white nuns, had left home at thirteen, and had been in the monastery for eighteen years. Lawrence Lucas, a radical priest from New York who spent some time in Indianapolis during the 1960s, talked about how black men were "whitened" during their education in Catholic schools and seminaries of that era.[39] Bill Hardin echoed this effect in talking about the Ursuline sisters who taught the Hardin brothers in school: "Some of them were very young and came from the deep South and a lot of the times some of these racial mores hung on some of these young ladies as they came through. And the idea that we were colored still stuck with some people that we were less than other people."[40] Many of these sisters felt that educating black children meant changing their language and cultural habits and values. As an obedient and conscientious student, young Randy would have been highly susceptible to the sisters' acculturation efforts.

Indianapolis in the 1960s, however, was not the monastery, and Father Hardin was immediately thrown into a brew of police brutality, neighborhood crime and poverty, de facto segregation, and a white Church establishment hesitant to combat these problems. He later reflected: "Having lost the security of a daily schedule, companionship of people who seemed to think like me, or at least to have a common goal of God and love in the monastic environs, I found myself confronted by the wiles of the world filled with so much confusion." He wondered, "How in the world was I to convert the world from paganism to God? Besides, being black, I was somehow supposed to quicken the process of evangelization of my people to Catholicism. It was all very frightening. The only answer I came up with was Jesus: Do what he did." Father Hardin talked about how his role developed to include other forms of support in addition to the spiritual: "Jesus lived among his own people, ate with them, suffered and rejoiced. That was to be my goal, too, but that was a lot harder done than said. The demands of parish responsibilities were overwhelming, but I made every effort to respond to the needs of the people. Soon, food, clothing, liturgy, home visits, potholes and trash in the streets, became one."[41]

As he worked within the parish neighborhood, Father Hardin's natural gregariousness and empathy caused him to want to help. His background as a black man realizing anew the injustices of racism emerged in the form of both anger and racial pride. Referring particularly to the attempts to perpetuate school segregation in Indianapolis, Smith recalled, "So those kinds of activities taking place infuriated Boniface a little more. That was his education to the real world. Instead of the monastery, instead of just praying. He says there really is racism. I mean, it's enacted by official bodies like school boards. like city councils, etcetera."[42] Some years later, Father Hardin wrote about this: "Holy Angels was a part of my learning process as a priest and as a black man. I learned what I could and could not do . . . I had to learn to deal with a parish. I had been a bookkeeper, but I wanted to work with my people as a priest."[43]

Father Hardin's sense of mission was not entirely embraced by his fellow priests. He recalled later that he was "reminded by my elders—priests who were older and always knew better—that the work of the priest is not social work, but attending to the needs of the parishioners: [They said] 'If you wanted to do social work, you should have become a social worker. A priest should take care of the spiritual needs of his people, not their physical needs.'"[44] He became more and more aware of the ways in which the Catholic Church was complicit in the racism of the times. Smith observed, "For Boniface to witness this interaction between good, down home, loving, living Catholics who happened to be black, and to see that their religious faith and belief was being challenged just because of their ethnicity, it put him in a tizzy. And I think he was constantly learning more and more how racist and degrading the behaviors of the powers that be were, and the Catholic Church because the Catholic schools were segregated."[45]

Father Hardin also became aware of how his association with the Catholic Church potentially hampered his civil-rights efforts within Indianapolis and especially within the black community. "The biggest disappointment that I've had in Indianapolis has been its religious bigotry," he said. "I came as a Catholic priest to Holy Angels and I wore my little tiny collar and I looked like a Catholic priest. . . . I got into the community and found that I was not a leader because I was a Catholic. But the other preachers were leaders so I said, 'Okay, if that's the rules of the game,' I took off my collar and was like everybody else. . . . And so the result was that I got to know people and found out they thought that Catholic priests were sort of snooty . . . I wasn't going to let that get in the way. I won some of their hearts over."[46] For the remainder of his life, Father Hardin downplayed public manifestations of his Catholicism and, through constant close association with key religious leaders from many religions, developed a strong belief in ecumenism that thoroughly informed his actions.

One of the first undertakings for Father Hardin in the community was the founding of the Northwest Action Council. In establishing the council, Father Hardin and his colleagues hoped to understand more deeply the local area and its needs. With the help of several parish and community members, Father Hardin led a project to conduct a survey of the northwest area of Indianapolis. Sixty-seven students from nearby Marian College were enlisted to complete interviews of more than a thousand families. The report focused on the geographic area and its demographics, the families, economic issues, churches, schools, community associatiations, recreation and culture, and crime.[47] The findings documented the breakdown of family structures and increases in sexual diseases, crime, and unemployment. The report asserted that major industries were abandoning the area, churches and ministers were "indifferent" toward the needs of the community, schools were overcrowded, and recreational facilities for youth were lacking.[48]

The NAC followed up on the situation described in the report and brought together community organizations and advocates to begin its work in 1966.

The council formed subcommittees to deal with each of the themes in the report. From the start, Father Hardin's attention to broad involvement was apparent: among the speakers at the first meeting were protestant ministers in the area, leaders of community associations, the mayor of Indianapolis, the archbishop, and other public officials. The NAC disseminated the report to business and religious leaders in the area, as well as political leaders and school officials. The organization issued widespread calls for participation in the new association.

As an example of the NAC's modest beginnings, a letter to William E. Schaefer from Father Hardin on February 28, 1967, contained an appeal for $19.10 for incorporation fees, $7.80 for stationery, and $25.00 for stamps and paper. Father Hardin concluded, "We will succeed, if I have anything to do with it—but I need your financial help now. Please, Sir, if it's only to cover the Incorporation needs, we would appreciate it so much.[49]

FATHER BONIFACE HARDIN COLLECTION, INDIANA HISTORICAL SOCIETY

Father Hardin began growing an Afro while he was associate pastor of Holy Angels Church, Indianapolis, around 1969.

Despite its humble beginnings, the NAC was quite active in its first year, beginning with social and cultural activities and support for the move of Flanner House, a community center, to a new location. The council also sponsored a forum for four mayoral candidates to speak to the community and began involvement in a major issue for the area at the time: the planned building of I-65 (an interstate highway) through the neighborhood.[50]

Newspaper notices and photos during this period at Holy Angels showed Father Hardin in his priestly role—officiating at marriages and funerals, saying Mass, accepting checks for the parish from the women's Sodality group, and organizing a neighborhood cleanup day with a local neighborhood minister. Father Hardin joined the board of the Community Action Against Poverty organization and was appointed by the mayor to a task force to study the needs of low-income blacks.[51] He became a fixture in Holy Angels Parish and began to be widely recognized in the community. Gradually, he changed the style of his appearance to resemble black activists of the time. He wore dashikis and grew a substantial Afro. The activities he implemented included parading through the neighborhood with the Holy Angels drum-and-bugle corps and leading the local March on Poverty when King came to Indianapolis. Father Hardin wrote, "I became very involved in the civil rights movement. I just followed where the need was.[52]

Smith recalled this transformation: "Father Boniface was becoming more aware of his blackness, is the way I would say it. . . . But keeping in mind during these times, we were just beginning to realize the essence of, you know, black pride. We all had big Afros, black power kind of things. And seeking social justice. And I think that all that overwhelmed Father Boniface. Mind you, he was in a cloister down at Saint Meinrad's.[53]

Father Hardin was visible and respected by the youth of the neighborhood, through his presence on playgrounds where he was called to break up fights or on the street corners that he patrolled regularly. Paul Washington Lacey, a former Holy Angels youth, remembered that Father would approach the gangs on the basketball court at Holy Angels and just give them "the look," which was enough to make them behave.[54] Parishioner Billie Glenn recalled that Father Hardin would go to areas where the gangs hung out and try to calm them by talking to them and trying to keep peace in the area so that people were not hurt. "And that was a very unsafe area to be in if you didn't know the people there at that time because everybody was angry," she noted.[55] An example of Father's approach with young people is found in his response to the burning of a local grocery by the neighborhood youth. To demonstrate the consequences of the arson, he chose to have the meeting and discussion inside the charred remains of the store, which was never replaced—a great inconvenience for the community.[56] In another incident, he called upon a local youth to serve as the go-between in an incident that could have led to a street fight and developed this recruited peacemaker, Clete Ladd, into a community leader.[57]

Gardner, who lived in the Holy Angels area at the time, spoke of Father Hardin's work with the gangs and his monitoring of police activity: "I would say that was his whole introduction to what he was going to do later because then he took on not only fighting the police department, the injustice of it, he began to see more injustice that was being done in the neighborhood and he would always talk to us about it and then he would have these rallies and things that he would get together and we would all go to."[58] As activities escalated, tension between the black community and the police and public officials increased. Smith, who had taken on leadership roles in the struggle, portrayed a scene where retribution against black activists was swift and often hidden. His friends in the police department often patrolled his neighborhood to ensure his safety.[59]

Father Hardin's alliances with other local ministers and community organizers made him a popular and familiar figure at demonstrations. A key focus of their efforts was influencing the plan for construction of I-65 through the northwest neighborhood surrounding Holy Angels. This was only one branch of the construction of interstate highways in Indianapolis that was to displace as many as 20,000 people in densely populated neighborhoods.[60] Monsignor Joseph Reidman, who served at Holy Angels from 1956 to 1960, remembers that surveyors were canvassing the area around the church as early as the mid-1950s.[61] The choice was between construction through the black neighborhood or the nearby wealthier white area and Crown Hill Cemetery.

When the path through the Holy Angels neighborhood had been chosen, a key report called for a "depressed" highway to be built so that street traffic and existing housing would not be greatly disturbed. Indiana governor Roger Branigin and Indianapolis mayor John Barton were initially in favor of this plan.[62] In time, however, the original idea was shelved in favor of a cheaper street-level alternative that bisected the neighborhood and caused the loss of many homes. Since such construction in urban neighborhoods at the time frequently disrupted poor, black areas, rather than adjacent wealthier white areas, the I-65 issue became one associated with race and poverty. Smith remembered the resentment in the black community: "Our observation was, well they are just trying to destroy all these black families, black homes. . . . And of course the thinking in the black community is, well, they are going to bring this highway through here because they can just uproot all these black folk and don't care."[63]

Assisted by Sister Jane, Father Hardin and others canvassed the Holy Angels neighborhood and distributed yard signs protesting the highway, accompanied by Sister's drum-and-bugle corps. They would find that the signs disappeared quickly, and they repeated the process numerous times, generating more participation and awareness each time.[64]

In 1967 Father Hardin and his clerical and lay associates, chiefly a parishioner named Doctor Robert Treadwell, presented petitions to Barton and to the city council calling for the depressed design.[65] Parents in the affected area met with the Indianapolis Public School board, arguing about safety conditions that would arise with the construction of the proposed highway, as well as school overcrowding issues.[66] Having not had a response on the petitions from the mayor, Father Hardin and the group met with Branigin, who provided some support.[67] Later in the year, however, the new mayor, Richard Lugar, said he would appeal to the governor for a depressed design only if he felt there would be support from the affected citizens.[68] Doctor Pat Treadwell recalled her father's recounting of a meeting with the mayor, during which the group argued for the depressed design out of safety considerations. Both Robert Treadwell and Father Hardin came back enraged. "I vividly remember my father saying that the answer from Mayor [Richard] Lugar was, 'We don't get the black vote, we don't need the black vote. We're going to put I-65 wherever we want to put it,'" recalled Pat Treadwell.[69]

In 1968 the NAC filed suit to mandate the choice of the depressed design, and CORE passed a resolution supporting the design in February.[70] Lugar maintained that it was too late to change the design for a street-level construction, and the governor did not comment or intervene.[71] Father Hardin was quoted about these developments in the *Indianapolis Recorder*, the paper that serves the city's black community: "I would say the basic issue is bigger than the highway. It is trust in government and true concern for the poor. The Negro community has been told by government officials to stand by them and they would try to help them. However, in the next breath they say something different or do not stand behind the people. They are talking double-tongued to us. The people are given something to riot for by public officials with such pre-emptory attitudes. It is a serious problem."[72]

Meanwhile, other issues were continuing to boil over in the northwest community, one of which caused a furor that led to a major turning point in Father Hardin's life. In February 1969 the Shortridge "incident" occurred. It involved the disciplining of a student who wore a Black Power t-shirt to school. For years Shortridge High School had been the site of a struggle for racial integration. Repeated actions to effectively keep the student population white had been enacted over the years, including the institution of an entrance exam. Students who did not pass the exam were bused to another Indianapolis high school. The Black Panthers had just come to Indianapolis and protests were rampant. In the midst of this tense climate, the situation at Shortridge escalated. Students rampaged through the building, protesting the disciplinary action in the t-shirt incident.

On the following day, Shortridge students presented demands to the school administration. Feeling that the response was inadequate, twenty-three students marched out during a school concert. Reverend Luther Hicks and several adult supporters assisted them in organizing the demonstration outside of the school. Father Hardin was one of the clerics who addressed the assembled students. The police response was swift and severe. Theodore Boyd, a protestor who watched as police dragged students down the school stairs, described the incident as one of the "most brutal things I've ever witnessed in my life."[73] Seven adults and twenty-three students were arrested. Although the school board opted to drop charges, the local prosecutor moved to have the students appear in criminal rather than juvenile court. Leaders of the Black Coalition, a group of ten organizations cochaired by Father Hardin and Reverend Gerald Cunningham, protested and developed a proposal for a ten-point program to address racial issues in the Indianapolis schools. Although Father Hardin was not among those arrested, his engagement in the incident was used in a purported attempt by the Indianapolis Police Department to have him removed from his post at Holy Angels.

There are conflicting details about the attempted removal. Community members and the local news coverage at the time are consistent in detailing allegations that some member of the police force contacted Paul C. Schulte, the Archbishop of Indianapolis, to tell him that Father Hardin was a threat to the community and must be removed from his position.[74] Smith later recalled in a 2012 radio interview that the police chief told the Archbishop that Father Hardin was brought to Indianapolis not "to be a rebel rouser [rabble-rouser], just to take care of the coloreds."[75] Lugar's office denied that the administration knew of any action on the part of a police official to have Father Hardin removed. In a private letter to Father Hardin, Lugar claimed no complicity but said that a police chaplain had been involved.[76] Father Hardin's reaction was quoted in the *Recorder*: "When the police department thinks it can pressure religious authority to dispose of a man in one way or another it hits at the whole relationship between church and state. If the voice of a spokesman who speaks out against injustice is muffled, this creates a gap for communication. I don't think the thing has been resolved in my own mind or conscience, both church-wise and civilly."[77]

Accounts of Archbishop Schulte's reactions also vary, yet private letters from Father Hardin to his superior at Saint Meinrad, Archabbot Gabriel Verkamp, reveal that Archbishop Schulte did indeed inform Father Hardin on

March 13, 1969, that he was no longer to serve at Holy Angels.[78] In later recalling the archbishop's request that Archabbot Verkamp summon him to return to the abbey, Father Hardin said that his immediate response was "'Hey, that's wrong, that's immoral, because what I'm standing up for is what I'm supposed to be standing up for and you're going to go along with these people.' 'Well, [I was told by the archabbot], just keep calm, you know, and you['ll] come back.'"[79]

Father Cyprian Davis remembered that Father Hardin was indeed recalled to the abbey but refused to go. He indicated that this refusal was thought to be against Father Hardin's vow of obedience but that the archabbot did not want to force the issue, fearing that Father Hardin would leave the order, so he levied a punishment that Father Davis felt was unjust—Father Hardin was not allowed to meet the first black cardinal in the church who was visiting at the time.[80] Father Davis recalled that the monks were split in their opinions about Father Hardin. Some felt he was a prophet and were very supportive of his efforts, while others thought that his activities were inappropriate for a monk. Father Hardin was extremely chagrined that he was never allowed to answer the charges made against him.

Fellow priests, parishioners, and local organizations responded forcefully when they learned of the actions against Father Hardin. Reverend Donald M. Clark, President of the Black Catholic Clergy Caucus, sent Archbishop Schulte a letter from the caucus in which he wrote: "The action taken against Father Boniface, though it was carefully kept from general public view, makes the Church in your Archdiocese less credible as a center of justice, and, even more seriously, if offers the very clear implication that the Church will subject even its most committed men to harassment, intimidation and occult discipline when these suit Its purpose. And because the matter of race is clearly the basis for Father Boniface's removal, it is evident that the Catholic Church in Indianapolis is not really willing to root out racism in itself nor to be more than 'an uncertain trumpet' in the community."[81] In addition, Father Bernard Strange, who, as pastor of Saint Rita Church and a great fund-raiser, wielded a great deal of influence in the archdiocese, reportedly interceded on Father Hardin's behalf.[82] Word of brewing opposition reached Archbishop Schulte, who quietly rescinded his order.

On March 26, 1969, Father Hardin sent a letter to Archabbot Verkamp, recounting the events connected with his removal and reinstatement, voicing a sense of betrayal:

Dear Father Archabbot Gabriel:

On Thursday, March 13, 1969, in the Holy Angels Rectory, 740 West 28th Street, Indianapolis, Indiana, the following declaration was made:

1. That the Most Reverend Paul C. Schulte, Archbishop of Indianapolis, demanded the immediate dismissal of Reverend Father Boniface Hardin, OSB, Associate Pastor of Holy Angels Church.
2. That the Police Department of Indianapolis said that Reverend Father Boniface Hardin, OSB, had directly or indirectly caused the students of Shortridge High School, Indianapolis, Indiana, to riot or demonstrate.
3. That the Police Department of Indianapolis said that Reverend Father Boniface Hardin, OSB, was being used by certain groups, i.e. Black organizations, and that he was detrimental to the racial condition of the city of Indianapolis.

In reference to the above accusations, the Reverend Father Boniface Hardin, OSB, made the following observations:

1. That involvement in the Black parish means involvement with people and their problems, and this includes Black organizations.
2. That a speech had been given to an assembly of students at Shortridge High School and that he had advised the students, together with their parents, to resolve their grievances with the school administration.
3. That the Police Department was eager to rid the city of a strong voice advocating professional policemen and protesting Police brutality inflicted on the citizens. Numerous examples were given.
4. That this dismissal would be disastrous for the Church of Indianapolis, since the move was prompted by the Police Department, an agency which has alienated a large segment of the community, particularly the Black community.

Since the declaration of March 13, 1969, the accused subject was informed by the Reverend Albert Ajamie, Pastor of Holy Angels Church, on March 15, 1969, that the Right Reverend Archabbot Gabriel Verkamp, OSB concurred with the Most Reverend Archbishop Paul C. Schulte in the recension of the immediate dismissal for an indefinite period. Numerous communications were made with the Police Department to affect this reversal. Since there has been no communication to the contrary, the above verbal concurrence will remain effective.

Since the Reverend Father Boniface Hardin, OSB was judged, condemned, and ordered to leave the city, it is the opinion of many learned and holy people:

1. That one of the most basic of all human rights, namely, that one is innocent until proven guilty, has been violated.
2. That the most elemental of Christian virtues, Charity, was ignored.
3. That the dignity and fraternity of the priesthood was made meaningless.
4. Restitution must be made as expeditiously as the damage was incurred.

It is the opinion of the experienced and conscientious people, clerical and lay, Black and White, Catholic, Protestant, and Jewish:

1. That the Catholic Church is truly guilty of that racism condemned by the Black Priests Caucus of April, 1968.
2. That the Archdiocese of Indianapolis has created a public scandal in the Church.
3. That such a censure without recourse has served as an intimidation to Reverend Father Boniface Hardin, OSB and to all the priests in the Archdiocese.
4. That Reverend Father Boniface Hardin, OSB has expressed fear of harassment from the Indianapolis Police Department.

It is the opinion of the undersigned that by reason of the failure of the Right Reverend Archabbot of Saint Meinrad to question of the truth of the accusations, he has been compromised by the Most Reverend Paul C. Schulte, and has betrayed the condemned subject.[83]

Below his signature, Father Hardin added the names of a number of individuals to be copied: Archbishop Schulte; Father Ajamie; Reverend Rollins Lambert, chairman of the Black Catholic Clergy Caucus; the pastors of Little Flower Parish and Saint Rita Parish (Father Raymond Bosler and Father Strange); three members of the Priests Association of Indianapolis (Reverend Robert Walpole, president Reverend Richard Mode, member of the Personnel Board, and Reverend Kenny Sweeney, member of the board of governors); and, finally, his parents, Albert and Elizabeth Hardin.

Parishioners were assured by Father Ajamie, on March 29, 1969, that the effort to remove Father Hardin had failed and that rumors that he would be reassigned during the annual assignment of priests in May were unfounded.[84] Father Hardin later recalled his feelings at the time: "The agony of the entire episode was the damage it did to my Mom, Dad, brothers and me, the irreparable damage to my role as priest in the Church, and the scandal to all people. In the end, when the decision was reversed to allow me to stay in Indianapolis, there were no apologies, only pretenses to the effect that it did not happen at all."[85]

In spite of the reinstatement of Father Hardin, lingering resentment of the incident, coupled with complaints of the treatment of black Catholics within the Church, galvanized the Concerned Black Catholics group, which wrote to Archbishop Schulte presenting a list of ten grave concerns and a call for the holding of a diocesan synod to further discuss the issues.[86] Strong recalled that in a meeting with the archbishop, the group felt that he had been rude to the organization, belittled its ideas, and refused to fund its requests or its organization.[87] Fueled by anger, the group met at Strong's home, convening parishioners, and with the help of Reverend Hicks, a well-known civil rights activist, attracted many others in the community.

At the meeting the Concerned Black Catholics decided on a course of action, organizing a highly publicized walkout during a Mass officiated by Archbishop Schulte in Saints Peter and Paul Cathedral on Easter Sunday, April 6, 1969. The protesters planned to insert letters of discontent into the collection basket and to disrupt the Mass by filing out silently during the service.[88] The protest was enacted dramatically according to plan and was so effective that many worshipers who were not part of the group rose and exited the cathedral, thinking that the procession was part of the service. The *New York Times*, as well as the local press and various Indiana papers, reported on the turmoil that ensued.[89] Members of the group took care not to involve Father Hardin in the walkout to prevent further retribution toward him. Smith, the group's spokesman, said in a prepared statement that the walkout was an attempt "to inform the Easter weekend Christian community of the injustice which exists in the Catholic church of Indianapolis under the leadership of Archbishop Schulte." He indicated that the group was also specifically concerned with the case of Father Hardin, claiming, "This particular priest represented a real Christian ideal to many poor of our community. . . . We demand that any charges against any priest be conducted with respect for the dignity and office of the priesthood, that accused priests be given an equal chance to be heard." The Concerned Catholics' statement concluded that the protest was staged "because the institutional church has repeatedly failed to respond to the major problems of racism, war, poverty and technology in our society. We flatly refuse to stand by and see priests being exploited.[90]

Throughout the remainder of 1969, Father Hardin continued to pursue the highway construction as well as other social justice issues. He protested

Father Hardin meets with Indianapolis mayoral candidate Richard Lugar (second from right), Reverend Andrew Williams (right), and Reverend James Odom (left), in 1967.

the mayor's absence at a forum held at nearby Watkins Park in July: "It is disconcerting to us that Mayor Barton was not able and did not come to speak to this community as 'father' of the community. We did not invite him as a politician but to come to hear his people."[91] Later, the group organized a cavalcade to drive from Holy Angels Church to the mayor's office with petitions containing some 3,000 signatures urging the use of a depressed design for the highway.

Father Hardin's connections with the national scene, including various marches, had been consistent. He became a familiar figure, with the other black ministers in the Indianapolis fight for civil rights, known to Reverend Jesse Jackson, King, and other key national activists. Under Sister Jane's leadership, Holy Angels students participated in voter registration campaigns and decorated vehicles to take part in the poverty march that came through Indianapolis in 1968 as part of the Poor People's Campaign; those in the drum-and-bugle corps paraded with muffled drums around Monument Circle in the center of downtown Indianapolis.[92]

Father Hardin spoke at numerous rallies against poverty and in late July joined protests against the killing of an eighteen-year-old unarmed youth who was driving a stolen car in the neighborhood. This was the second time in 1969 that a black youth had been shot by the police.[93] He continued to experience opposition from the established leaders in the city and in the Church and later reflected on this: "The Seminary and Monastery did not teach me to be a leader, nor the correct thing to say in front of a community meeting or a television. It was almost unheard of, that a priest would disagree with a public servant, or even become angry in public. . . . However, I knew that my people had found a voice in me, and I hung on. The tension to be 'a good priest' as the words were understood, and to imitate Christ as I saw Him, were, in some ways, in conflict."[94]

Father Hardin found it hard to understand the reluctance of the Catholic Church to intervene in social-justice issues, such as police brutality within the black community. He said, "Time and time again, Black youths were stopped and frisked. If they ran, they were shot down in cold blood. When it happened in our neighborhood, on the west side of Indianapolis in 1969, I called the policeman a murderer. My priestly colleagues reminded me not to judge: After all, the policeman was an interpreter of justice."[95] Undaunted, Father Hardin later filed and won a federal lawsuit against police actions in Indianapolis and began to consult with the Indiana General Assembly on police behavior.[96]

As the years passed, it became clear that the highway would not be depressed, causing Father Hardin to reflect, "In looking back, I think we did some good about the highway. There were some things that were modified as a result of our protests, and we got them to leave some homes they had planned to take."[97] Yet, he clearly was seeking new direction. Gardner recalled a critical incident in Father Hardin's decision making. As she was standing on the back stairs of Holy Angels School with Sister Jane, Father Hardin returned from a meeting with the police department downtown. Gardner remembered, "He said, 'This is it.' You know, no longer could he be, he had to do something more than being associate pastor going from parish to parish. He said, 'This is it.' So Sister Jane and I just kind of looked, like 'Okay, like what are you going to do now?' He said, 'I don't know, but I'm doing something, this is it. You know, I can't do it in the setting that I'm in.'"[98]

During this same period, a group called the National Black Catholic Clergy Caucus came to Father Hardin's attention. The organization first met in Detroit in April 1968 with fifty-eight priests, one brother, and one nun in attendance. (The sisters were urged to form their own organization, which they did in August 1968.) The attendees talked about the present state of black Catholics and the formation of an organization within the church to take special responsibility for opening the Church to African Americans as well as advocating for the cause of blacks in general. A major difference concerning the issue of violence was the focus of considerable discussion. While some priests argued that violence was necessary for social change, others supported nonviolence.[99]

In the statement issued following the meeting, several demands were made, including that there be a black priest in decision-making positions on the diocesan level and in the black community, that efforts to recruit black men to the priesthood be stepped up, and that a specific department and funding be developed within the Church structure for supporting the black struggle for freedom and fighting racism.[100] The statement called on U.S. bishops to respond.

In July Father Hardin was invited through a mass mailing to all the black Catholic priests from Father Lambert, newly elected chair of the BCCC, to attend the group's meeting in November 1968 in Washington, DC. Following this meeting, Father Lambert and the Executive Committee of the BCCC wrote to Archbishop John Dearden, president of the National Conference of Catholic Bishops, expressing frustration that the bishops had not responded to the group's April statement and warning that they would escalate their work with or without the bishops' sanction.[101]

Meanwhile, a regional group of black priests from the Midwest, coordinated by Father Don Clark of Detroit, scheduled a meeting in Chicago on December 8 to support the BCCC. Father Hardin attended this meeting.[102] On the national level, the bishops' organization responded to the April BCCC statement by appointing a liaison committee to meet with the BCCC; a meeting was held in January 1969. At this meeting, one main demand was made—that the Church set up a secretariat to focus on the needs of black Catholics.[103]

Following the first meeting with the BCCC on January 30, 1969, the bishops set up an ad-hoc committee to further explore the group's ideas. The BCCC executive committee then met and developed a formal proposal for a central office, rather than a secretariat, and outlined its goals for the bishops in a March 1969 meeting. The liaison committee responded positively and the proposal was brought to the NBCCC meeting in Houston in April 1969. The ad-hoc committee was directed to work with the NCCB to further refine the proposal.[104]

At its second national meeting in April 1969, the main topics were the establishment of the central office and the constitution for the BCCC. A meeting with the bishops was scheduled for May. In November the BCCC met again to further refine the proposal and constitution. In addition to the development of a central office, the establishment of regional groups was recommended.[105] In November the NCCB approved the establishment of the central office.

As Father Hardin participated in the early activities of the BCCC, a vision for his next steps emerged. By the end of May 1969 he had developed a proposal for the Central Office for Black Catholicism in the United States. The main purposes of this organization would be: To define and provide guidelines for the bishops and other ecclesiastical authorities in facing the racial crisis, described by the bishops as "unprecedented in the history of the nation or of the Church"; to bring more effectively into operation the resources of the Church as found particularly in black priests, religious of both sexes, and laity; to witness the catholicity of the Church by recognizing and utilizing the potential for leadership in the black community; to make genuine black control and leadership effective within the Catholic Church in the black community; and to develop new types of ministries originating in black communities, and to review other types of ministries proposed for the black community.[106] The proposal outlined training programs for parish renewal, white priests, sisters, and laity; and leadership training for black laity. It proposed at least four regional centers to be operation bases for training teams and programs. The central office would be funded by appropriations from the NBCCC and nationwide annual parish collections.[107]

In a subsequent document, coauthored by Father Hardin and the Very Reverend Bernardin Patterson, OSB, Conventual Prior of Saint Maur's Priory, the objectives of the Central Office on the Church in Indianapolis were enumerated: The Priests, Sisters, and Brothers working in the Black community will receive intense training in the culture and mores of Black people; leadership training programs for Black laity will be initiated; cooperation will be given to the Social Action Director to eradicate racism in suburbia; relevant programs will be innovated to meet the needs of the people; and the Church will become a visible sign of love to all people—particularly the Black people.[108]

On June 13, 1969, Father Hardin participated in a panel presentation at the regional meeting of the BCCC. In his outline for the talk, he pointed out that the Church in America maintained slaves and instituted a pattern of segregation in churches, seminaries, convents, and schools. Father Hardin's remarks emphasized that the Church discouraged black men and women from entering the religious life and its bishops only spoke out against racism after actions of the US government and the Supreme Court had already sanctioned it. He recommended that funds should be allocated for inner-city Catholics for schools, parishes, job training, housing development, health programs, and training for priests, sisters, and laity. He concluded, "Unless there is an honest evaluation of the Church and the Black community, followed with a genuine moral and financial support, the Church will be free of its Black Christians and Black priests."[109]

In late summer Father Hardin conducted a study of the needs of black people within the Church and in Indianapolis specifically, culminating in a refined proposal for action. In the study he warned that black Catholics were not finding a home compatible with their spirituality and would continue to leave the Church unless changes were made. He proposed small liturgies in homes, an increase in black priests, liturgical ceremonies rooted in black culture, and deacons or catechumens living in neighborhoods among the people. Black priests would have leadership within the Church structure.[110] He shared his proposal with several others during the next several months of 1969. It appears that he had hopes that the center he was proposing in Indianapolis would be the basis for the central office being discussed by the BCCC. As the months went by, it became apparent that there was little support for locating the national central office in Indianapolis; consequently, the proposal became more local in its orientation and the goal shifted to the development of a regional center affiliated with the national center. Father Hardin began to call this regional center the Martin Center, a name that would be explained more fully once the center came into existence. At the end of October 1969, Father Hardin discussed his future plans in a letter to his superior, Archabbot Verkamp:

> As you know, I have strong convictions about the need for the Church to witness by action what It says with words to the Black people. My first consideration was to ask for a pastorate which would put me in an honorable position in the Black community. As you know, the Black [Catholic] Clergy Caucus does not favor Black priests being under a non-Black priest in the Black community. It is my feeling and the feeling of others, such as Abp. Mc-Donough of Louisville, that a Black priest should be in a leadership position among his own people. However, certain things have come to my atten-

tion indicating that this is not a real possibility for me in the Archdiocese. Furthermore, it is my conviction and the counsel of others that my energy and talent can best be served to the advantage of my people and the good of the Church by seeking to establish Martin Center in Indianapolis. . . . It is my hope that you will permit me to pursue this apostolate as outlined in the proposal. This, of course, means that I will work full time at Martin Center and terminate my duties as Associate Pastor at Holy Angels Church.[111]

Father Hardin wrote letters to all members of the bishop's ad-hoc committee reviewing the BCCC proposal and to members of the executive committee seeking their endorsement for the Martin Center. The central office proposed by the BCCC had been approved by the bishops and Father Hardin continued to work on the specifics of his plan for Martin Center. In a letter to Warren Atkinson, of Atkinson and Company Real Estate, he described his idea and asked Atkinson to donate a building he owned at 404 East 38th Street to the Black Catholic Clergy Caucus "for the explicit purpose of combating racism in Indianapolis and to be used as a training center for people who will work in the inner city."[112] Thus prepared, Father Hardin attended the national meeting of the BCCC in November in Techny, Illinois, to further propose policy for the central office. His hope was that the Martin Center would be a local affiliate of the central office; however, his request was turned down for lack of funding.[113]

Father Kenneth Taylor, former pastor of Holy Angels Church and Saint Rita Parish and past president of the NBCCC (the organization eventually came to be called the National Black Catholic Clergy Caucus) recalled an additional reason for the reluctance of the BCCC to endorse the Martin Center. At the time, various groups were coming to the NBCCC seeking its endorsement for projects they were implementing in their dioceses. By the time Father Hardin made his proposal, the caucus decided that there needed to be a more formal process for judging the worth of projects submitted for endorsement. The delay irritated Father Hardin. Father Taylor remembered, "And so they didn't [endorse the Martin Center], and that really discouraged [Father Hardin], and as a result he never came back to the Clergy Caucus."[114]

In a later letter to Bishop Harold Perry, member of the ad hoc bishops' committee, Father Hardin responded to what he perceived as the postponement of approval for local units in favor of first electing a national board and establishing the central office. He admonished the group for falling into what he regarded as a "common error" in dealing with black organizations—the need to create a national office before there were local ones. The approval of his own request, he felt, and that of Father Gus Taylor, who had proposed a local center in Steubenville, Ohio, would have spawned other centers. He argued, "That is water over the dam so we can forget it, but mind you, this is the common error of poverty programs, model city programs and job corps programs. The little people cannot believe in a group that has to have a national organization before it has a local one. So be it."[115]

Although he was troubled by the failure of the BCCC to support the establishment of the Martin Center, Father Hardin continued reworking his ideas and on December 5, 1969, sent a formal letter to his diocesan superior, Archbishop Schulte, arguing for the archbishop's support for the Martin Center. His expressed intention for a center separate from the central office advocated by the BCCC was based on his sense of urgency: "The Central Office will not exist even in germ for another six months and the actual development of the Office will not be actuated for at least another year or even a year and a half. For this reason, then, the proposed Martin Center cannot carry the title of Central Office for Black Catholicism."[116]

In his letter Father Hardin indicted that he had received permission from Archabbot Verkamp to work full time as the director of the Martin Center. He also related that he had commitments from two religious sisters to work full time at the center and that colleagues from the BCCC in Indianapolis would assist as well. He outlined the initial activities of Martin Center:

1. An analysis of Indianapolis and the Archdiocese in terms of the Black community and its relation to the White community;
2. A report of the analysis to the Ordinary [bishop];
3. Preparation for the training programs, which would include the acquisition of resource personnel and communication with religious Orders, parishes, and lay organizations; and
4. Planning of programs with White parishes, religious Orders, and organizations desiring to improve race relations.

On December 13, 1969, Father Hardin reported to Archabbot Verkamp that a meeting had been held with Archbishop Schulte and that he "offered his blessings to the project. He was more than interested and saw this as an opportunity to effect a better relationship between Blacks and Whites and to bring more members into the Church in the Black community." He confided that his pastor, Father Ajamie, "has told me in no uncertain terms he does not wish to discuss matters of this sort with me. I regret this and I am deeply hurt by this, but that is part of God's plan too I suppose."[117] In a draft of this letter, Father Hardin's language about negotiations with Father Ajamie was more pointed: "In the course of this discussion, Father Ajamie reflected certain opinions concerning Blacks and my position at Holy Angels. In view of this discussion, it is my considered opinion that my effective service at Holy Angels will be inhibited. Consequently, it is desirable that I terminate my residence here as soon as possible."[118]

By the end of the year, then, Father Hardin had resolved to leave Holy Angels. It was clear that he was always walking the edge with his superiors in the archdiocese and the archabbey. Although technically, he retained his appointment with the parish after the March removal attempt, he had definitely been warned to keep a low profile. His choices were clear: "This town—crazy, narrow, bigoted, mean, these are my people, this is my home now. And that's just what I wanted it to be about. Go back to the monastery . . . you know, my life would be wasted. So, I was permitted to stay. And instead of staying in a parish, where I would, you know, be towed under again or given another parish, I started thinking about Martin Center, where I could train other priests and nuns who worked in the black community. So that was my transition. That's what I wanted to do."[119]

Adamant that he wanted to remain a monk, Father Hardin cited his source of strength during this time of transition: "My main support during this period was my belief in, and my love for, Jesus. That the Church was not perfect was very clear, but what was also clear was the fact that the Church institution was not about to change its attitude toward Black people, Black priests or sisters." He revealed that he had been offered positions to pastor a large black church in Louisville, Kentucky, and to serve with a congressman in Washington, DC, but "No, the service which I felt was mine to do was Martin Center. Somehow, I felt all that I had experienced at Saint Meinrad, in parish life, and the '60's, would come to bear on this dream: it seemed to be part of God's plan."[120]

Father Hardin's intention to leave was quietly announced at the end of the year and he moved on without fanfare. In a December 31, 1969, letter that began, "My Dear Friends," he said his good-byes:

> On August 20, 1965 I came to Indianapolis to serve as Associate Pastor of Holy Angels Church. These years have afforded me the opportunity to spread the Faith and to strive for social reform in the city and state. We have been involved in fighting the Interstate Highway and police brutality. We have demonstrated, picketed, petitioned and pleaded with authorities to change their ways toward Black people. As a Black priest (and I am sure

some may not understand why I want to make a distinction but this is a fact now) I feel that I have a special obligation in the light of my experience to effect the kinds of changes needed in the Church and in our city toward the poor, Black and White alike.

In November of 1969 the National Conference of Catholic Bishops approved, per the request of the National Black Catholic Clergy Caucus, the Central Office for Black Catholics. At that time it was my hope that the Bishops would approve Martin Center as a part of the Central Office, but this was not a part of the plan. The term "Central Office" cannot be used until the National Board is elected. However, on December 12, 1969 Archbishop Schulte of Indianapolis approved and blessed the work of Martin Center. I received permission from my Abbot to serve as the Director of this program and he asked that I begin it immediately. Consequently, I moved out of the rectory of Holy Angels on December 26, 1969 and until our place is purchased I am residing at Saint Maur's Priory and have an office in another place. [listed phone numbers]

Perhaps you are curious to know what Martin Center is about. Martin Center will do the following things:

1. Train people who work in the Black community
2. Develop race education programs for suburban Whites
3. Develop meaningful ways of relating Church to Black people
4. Initiate, support and coordinate programs for Black people

Financial support for these programs will come from people who believe in me and the ideas proposed. No money has been forthcoming from the Catholic Archdiocese though the Episcopal Church is seeking to fund a large portion, if not all of the program. It is once in a lifetime that a person can begin such a work as Martin Center and I am appealing to you and to your friends to help me in this undertaking. I have enclosed a list of items needed for the Martin Center. Whatever you wish to contribute toward one item or the other will be used for just that and nothing else. I hope you will feel free to call me and ask questions if you care to do so and I hope that you will not forget Martin Center and myself in your prayers.

Asking God to bless you, I remain

Sincerely yours,

Rev. Father Boniface Hardin, OSB, Director of Martin Center[121]

Later, summing up his parish experience, he wrote: "I was an oxymoron. Here I was supposed to be preaching the Gospel on Sunday. I'm worrying about whether somebody's got trash that's not being picked up or whether some kid had an encounter with the Police Department or whether or not houses are being taken down because of a highway. People didn't think that was sin. But it is sin—it's unfairness. It was wrong, it was inequitable. I wasn't dealing with it in terms of sin—I was dealing with the outcome; people were being hurt."[122]

The next step for Father Hardin was to find a place for the Martin Center and to outline the mission and goals of his future work. Fortunately, his many supporters were ready to assist.

Chapter 3

THE MARTIN CENTER YEARS, 1969–77: A NEW VISION FOR SOLVING THE RACE PROBLEM

"I figured I was going to solve the race problem. I figured it would take me about 10 years. That's how naïve I was. I had it all organized; it was all here on paper. I was going to deal with religion. I had another religious leader, a white minister who was going to deal with the white community. It was very naïve, but it was important. We would do one-day workshops. I traveled all over the United States for eight years, and I thought that was the essence of what Doctor King wanted to do, to bring us together."[1]

As 1969 drew to a close, Father Boniface Hardin planned for new beginnings. It was an exciting but anxiety-ridden time. He had to find a place to live, locate a home for the Martin Center, and refine and adapt his ideas to what was practical. The story of the Martin Center and what followed in the life of Father Hardin was shaped by his strong sense of purpose and determination; as he seized opportunities and made critical adaptations, he brought his dreams to fruition.

Father Hardin's superior at the monastery, Archabbot Gabriel Verkamp, had suggested that either Father Bernard Strange, pastor of Saint Rita Church, or Father Bernardin Patterson from Saint Maur Priory might provide a place for Father Hardin to live after he left Holy Angels Parish.[2] Father Strange was known for his compassion for black people and was also a shrewd businessman who ran Bingo games and an operation called "the Catholic Pool." This lottery was highly successful and drew in enough money to enable Father Strange to wield nearly unquestioned power within the diocese. Initially, Father Hardin went to live at Saint Maur but then worked from a home that Father Strange owned near Fall Creek on the northwest side of Indianapolis, not far from Holy Angels. Father Hardin worked out of a room that was filled with mimeograph equipment and other things necessary for the operation of the Catholic Pool. The parishioners continued to take care of him. Holy Angels parishioner Joseph Smith recalled how his mother and other women from Holy Angels brought Father Hardin dinner, helped with his laundry, and ministered to his needs.[3]

To assist in the quest to find a physical location for the Martin Center, Father Hardin enlisted a group of prominent black citizens, including Doctor Frank Lloyd, Doctor Robert Briggs, Doctor Ray Pierce, and Frank James.[4] They became his think tank for raising funds and articulating the Center's mission. Others helped Father Hardin find a physical location for the Center. They drove around looking at properties and finally settled on a double at the corner of College Avenue and Thirty-Fifth Street, northeast of the Holy Angels neighborhood. At first, Father Hardin rented space in the house, but gradually, his supporters raised the money for a down payment toward the property's purchase.

Although Father Hardin lists December 15, 1969 (occasionally December 12, 1969), as the founding date for the Martin Center, he was at Holy Angels until December 31 of that year. The plan was on paper in 1969, yet the physical operation began sometime later in 1970. While the original idea for the Center focused on helping the Catholic Church to serve black Catholics more effectively through the training of priests and religious orders, Father Hardin soon broadened the mission considerably. As his farewell letter to the Holy Angels community stated, he envisioned the Center as a place where race-education programs would be available not only to the clergy and religious leaders, but also to suburban white people. In addition, he began to think of providing educational programs on black heritage to the African American community.[5] Father Hardin framed the basic goal of the Center as "reconciliation."[6]

The logo of the Martin Center was two loaves of bread and an open bible inscribed with "the Word of God." The following dedication was posted inside the Center's entrance: "Martin Center is dedicated to two Black men who were concerned about having bread on the tables of the poor: Martin de Porres and Martin Luther King, Jr. Both men based their lives and their actions upon the Master, for they knew that man does not live on bread alone, but on the Word of God."[7] Although later he indicated that in retrospect, he would have named the Center after Malcolm X and King. Father Hardin continued to use the Martin name alone.[8]

The life of Martin de Porres, a saint in the Catholic Church, paralleled in many ways the life of Father Hardin. Martin was born in Peru of a mother of African or Indian descent, rendering him unacceptable for his desired entrance into the priesthood, a hurdle that Father Hardin also faced. An advocate for social justice, de Porres dedicated his life to ministering to the poor and oppressed, and Father Hardin was embarking on the same ministry. The Catholic

Church regards de Porres as the patron saint of mixed-race people and social justice.[9]

Father Hardin's relationship with the second Martin, Doctor Martin Luther King Jr., began during his time at Holy Angels. Father Hardin and his colleagues were active in participating in marches and rallies organized by King. One story tells of the first meeting between the two men. King was to speak at an inaugural service of Mount Zion Apostolic Church in Indianapolis and was seated on the dais next to Reverend Andrew J. Brown when King suddenly appeared quite startled. Reverend Brown looked to see what King saw and whispered an explanation. The object of King's attention was Father Hardin walking down the aisle in his dashiki, dramatically punctuating every step with an African walking stick. Rosa Lee Brown, Reverend Brown's wife, remembered the effect: "You have to understand that Father Hardin is a big man, especially with his extravagant hair and long beard. He had a serious look in his eye and walked very slowly and sternly. It was so dramatic—if you could have seen the look on King's face and the church full of people—I'll never forget it. Whenever Doctor King was in town, he would always ask about Father Hardin. Doctor King always said that he embodied the boldness of the civil rights movement."[10]

Father Hardin in dashiki, February 1970.

The examples of both de Porres and King shaped many of the Center's original and continuing programs. To raise needed revenue, Father Hardin and his associates began to offer workshops on racial sensitivity for corporate and nonprofit organizations. This work took him across the country, as well as to nearby locations. He and his staff served such clients as Lilly Pharmaceuticals, Indiana Bell Telephone, New Jersey Bell Telephone, United Parcel Service, Citizens Gas, the Young Men's Christian Association, and the Boy Scouts of America.[11] In addition, the Center offered programs for schools and held on-site workshops for interested individuals and groups. For example, workers sponsored by the Comprehensive Employment and Training Act were sent to the Center to learn about racial awareness on the job.[12] In time, Saint Meinrad Seminary began to send seminarians for three- and four-week experiences in racial relations as part of their education.[13] One participant, Father Pat Doyle, recalled spending two summers at the Center, the first as a participant in the workshops and the second, as a staff member.[14] Additional revenue was received from small grants and rent from tenant organizations, such as a project of the Indianapolis Human Relations Consortium, which had special funding to help parents during the desegregation of Indianapolis Public Schools.[15]

Shortly after the Center was founded, Sister Jane Shilling received permission from her superiors to leave her post at Holy Angels to work at the Center. Even though she had arranged for another sister to serve as principal, her departure created a void that the other sisters had to fill. Sister Jane was the Center's first employee after Father Hardin. At first she continued to live in the Holy Angels Convent. Tension developed as the other nuns struggled to adjust to her absence in the school and as Sister Jane pushed for the teachers to change their ideas about how to serve black students.[16] In a letter addressed to her superior some fifteen years later, she recalled that after a period of time, she did not have the support of her fellow sisters at Holy Angels to continue this arrangement and was asked to find another place to live.[17]

At first, Sister Jane refused to move. As tension escalated between the new principal, Sister Bridget, and the new pastor, Father Clarence Waldron, on the Holy Angels side, and Sister Jane and Father Hardin on the Martin Center side, the parish council served Sister Jane with an eviction notice. This incident deeply troubled her. For many years she was bitter about her treatment at the hands of her religious community. Nevertheless, she followed Father Hardin's lead and did not renounce her community and remained a Sister of Saint Joseph of Carondelet. Without a place to live, she relied on the hospitality of supporters of the Center to put her up until rental funds and a place to stay were located.[18] Sister Jane quickly fell into the role of researcher, office manager, and organizational expert for the Center. While Father Hardin traveled, she was the main administrator for the institution.

One of the first brochures for the Center in 1970 indicated that it was a "biracial and ecumenical effort to overcome the polarization brought about by ignorance, injustice and hostility between blacks and whites in the metropolitan area of Indianapolis." It was described as a school, a forum, and an agency. As a school, its programs focused on black leadership and race education. As a forum, it was a place "where dialogue, learning, and confrontation can take place in controlled circumstances." As an agency, it strove to work with existing community programs concerned with racism and to establish new programs when necessary.[19]

By May 22, 1970, the Center's bylaws and incorporation papers were filed and signed by the members of its original board.[20] As initial race relationship workshops established the institution's reputation and provided some financial base, other funding was obtained. The Irwin Sweeney-Miller Foundation presented the first grant of $7,000, which was followed by an Indianapolis Foundation grant of $60,000 for general operations in July 1970, and a Lilly Endowment contribution of $40,000 in August of that year. The Center also received numerous church, corporate, and individual donations, as well as gifts of furniture, equipment, books, and food.[21] Smith recalled that his family donated five dollars each week, a practice that was likely followed by other Holy Angels families.[22] Father Hardin and Sister Jane watched expenses closely. Staff member Mynelle Gardner told the story of how she and Sister Jane had to hide the cost of a new desk from Father Hardin since they spent more on it than he would have thought appropriate.[23]

The original staff of the Center was listed as Father Hardin, director; Sister Jane, coordinator of race education; George Evans, coordinator of current affairs; and Reverend Roger Anderson, coordinator of church relations.[24] Open houses for community members and officials were held in August 1970 and programming began in the fall with race education and black studies courses.

A key approach used in the Center's educational offerings was termed "ethnotherapy" by Father Hardin and Sister Jane. Father Hardin defined ethnotherapy as "Healing of the nations . . . a composite method of alleviating the fear, ignorance, and guilt that shackles the spirits of White and Black alike in America (and other colors in other countries as well)."[25] He explained: "This concept was derived from two Greek words—*ethnos* (race) and *therapao* (healing), which means healing one's racial feelings."[26] Ethnotherapy combined academic and experiential learning with small-group counseling methods. The technique was intended to promote mutual exchange of information and generate new perspectives. High-interest texts, such as emancipation narratives, theories of liberation, and poetry and prose of racial freedom were examined critically to promote self-reflection, healing, and dialogue. One book that became required reading, especially in workshops for public school teachers and academics, was *Pedagogy of the Oppressed* by Paulo Friere, a Brazilian philosopher and educator, that has become a classic in teacher preparation. As Gardner recalled, Friere's book became a staple of workshops and later classes at Martin College/University as well because Father Hardin wanted people to understand "how being oppressed sometimes made you an oppressive person."[27] Freire's ideas on critical pedagogy were to become influential in the Center's educational foundations; ethnotherapy continued to be a feature of the approach used throughout Father Hardin's career as an educator.

Father Hardin and Sister Jane led the workshops, enlisting others as they needed additional help. Gardner talked about the experience of being called to take charge of a summer workshop for public-school teachers. When she expressed a lack of preparation, Sister Jane assured her that her life experience would carry her through. The confidence that Father and Sister placed in her enabled her to tackle this new task and eventually feel great pride in her success. "Sister Jane was the type of person that if you didn't have a talent, she found it in you, somewhere way down in, she would bring it out," said Gardner.[28] She recalled the way in which she worked with Sister Jane, saying that Sister would depict the history of racial oppression, which would anger all the participants, leaving her other workshop partners to turn the workshop toward a positive tone. Gardner depicted Father Hardin's style as dialogic: he would continually probe and ask questions to try to get at the heart of personal beliefs, self-image, anger, or other emotions. She described Father in his teaching role as a great listener. She said she told him, "'You listen to what I said. You listen and I haven't said it yet and you heard it.' He was really a gifted, deep thinker."[29] Participant Father Pat Doyle recalled Sister Jane as a superb teacher; both she and Father Hardin brought artifacts like slave chains to the sessions for emotional impact. When Sister Jane challenged a participant, Father Doyle recalled, she stayed with that person until they reached a level of understanding and comfort.[30]

Those who attended the early workshops at the Center have vivid recollections of the experience. Sister Pat Quinn, a former teacher at Holy Angels, remembered attending a series of workshops offered for teachers. Several in her group of eight white nuns had never taught or lived in a black community and the sessions were geared to developing knowledge of and respect for black culture, as well as exploring biases and assumptions about how white teachers should create supportive environments for black students. While some of the sisters were thirsty for the ideas, others were less receptive. One positive participant was startled to realize that when she shopped in Indianapolis, she looked among the black people at the stores as well as the white to see if she knew them—a habit she had never had until she began to teach primarily black children.[31] Pat Payne, a widely known and respected teacher and cultural diversity leader in Indianapolis Public Schools, recalled having been in a similar set of workshops with public-school teachers. For her, the experience was transformative, one that she views as central to her career and life: "I believe it was a six-week institute, on my history and culture, African American history and culture. And it had never been presented to me like this. It was life changing for me. I changed my whole way of teaching, of working with students and everything after I came out of there, because I learned the truth."[32]

Very soon, new components were added under the Martin Center's umbrella. The first was the Sickle Cell Center, established in 1971. This center came about as Sister Jane and Father Hardin worked with families affected by the disease. Finding that there were few resources for testing and education about sickle cell anemia, Father Hardin and Holy Angels Doctor Ray Pierce committed to address the problem and established the Indianapolis Sickle Cell Anemia Foundation. In January 1971 Pierce presented a talk at the Center about the disease and its disproportionate effect on black people. Pierce's talk was followed by five monthly lectures by local doctors and the distribution of educational pamphlets and releases to the media.

INDIANAPOLIS RECORDER COLLECTION, INDIANA HISTORICAL SOCIETY

Father Hardin (center) receives a check from Lilly Foundation vice president Thomas Lake (left), as Doctor Edward Hicks (right), director of the Sickle Center lab, looks on, October 30, 1971.

Original buildings, Martin Center and Sickle Cell Initiative, on College Avenue, Indianapolis.

By mid-1971 the Center acquired its second building at 3549 North College Avenue, just south of the original building, to house the sickle cell program. Free sickle cell tests were offered on Wednesdays and more than 1,500 were tested in the month of April alone. The Sickle Cell Center arranged for mobile units to augment testing that was done in the College Avenue location. By October 1971 the first volunteer initiatives to offer education on sickle cell anemia attracted $15,000 in support from the Lilly Foundation. This was followed in 1972 by a major federal grant of $1.7 million, dedicated primarily for research, and shared with the Indiana University School of Medicine. Doctor Pierce, chairman of the Indianapolis Sickle Cell Anemia Foundation, referred to the donations that preceded this grant: "If the donations of time and effort by volunteers as well as money for the first two years were calculated, that amount alone would be more than double the amount of the grant."[33]

The establishment of the Sickle Cell Center is a case that illustrates the typical approach Father Hardin took to new initiatives. It began with sensitivity to a need in the black community and was fueled by compassion and determination to do something. To supplement his lack of medical knowledge, Father Hardin assembled experts from the community and motivated them to contribute their time and energy to educate him and the community about sickle cell. Operating on a shoestring budget, he grew the initiative before seeking major funding. His faith that such significant tasks as articulating the problem, developing approaches, and enacting programs came through sheer determination and was an essential part of the development of both the Sickle Cell Center and the Martin Center itself. Such determination also marked the establishment of future initiatives.

One such initiative was the third component of the Martin Center—the Afro-American Institute, which was added in April 1972. The institute was a vehicle for research and education about African and African American history and culture, specializing in the role of the black man in Indiana.[34] It began as a resource for leadership education, as well as a place for offering courses in black heritage, communication skills, and current issues. The focus was on scholarship and pride in learning. Father Hardin addressed potential resentment against intellectuals, particularly those who stressed moderation on race issues, saying that the institute, "will include people who heretofore have been called 'Toms.' These trained people will talk with those within the black community. Credibility will be restored, if not internally, externally."[35]

In due fashion a new building on 3553 North College Avenue was purchased to house the institute. As Martin Center expanded physically, Gardner recalled trying to distract Father Hardin from seeing "For Sale" signs in the neighborhood, fearing expansion was happening too quickly. But he would not be deterred. The physical setting of the institute included a library, other resource materials, and museum-like exhibits with artifacts such as slave chains and photographs. The institute hosted exhibits from the Smithsonian Center, children's puppet shows about the Underground Railroad, and a black Santa Claus (Father Hardin) at Christmas. Under the direction of Father Hardin, staff members for the institute included William Spalding, Marsha A. K. Holman, Sister Jane, Ronald Strange, Cossetta Beaven, Margaret L. Means, Jean Jarrett, and Lois Kennedy.[36] Several of these staff members are listed in dual roles as Center staff in another publication of the center: Spalding as assistant director, Sister Jane as coordinator of education, Beaven as bookkeeper, Jarrett as receptionist, and Kennedy as coordinator of housekeeping.[37]

One issue that also came to the attention of Father Hardin and Sister Jane was the adoption of black children. To address this need, the Afro-American Institute provided resources on adoption and advocacy for well-planned adoptions. It later added an initiative on marriage preparation to help establish strong foundations for black families.

STEFANIE LEE COLLECTION

Father Hardin as Santa Claus, Martin Center, circa 1972.

Through the Afro-American Institute the staff of the Martin Center made systematic attempts to disseminate its work, develop other activities, and engage new participants and volunteers. Father Hardin was a central presence through three major vehicles—radio, a print journal, and television. He was the producer and cohost of a weekly radio program, *The Afro-American in Indiana*, which ran from 1971 to 1991 on WIAN, the local public schools station that eventually affiliated with National Public Radio. From 1973 to 1978 Father Harden served as editor of the *Afro-American Journal*. On television he was the producer and cohost of *Afro-American* for the public television station Channel 20 (now WFYI) from 1973 to 1979, and narrated two full-length documentaries, *The Kingdom Builders* and *For Love of Freedom*, for WRTV, the local NBC affiliate.[38] Sister Jane cohosted several of these initiatives and was the key researcher for the information used in these productions.

The Afro-American in Indiana featured a variety of topics about history and current events and often centered on an interview with guests such as public officials or artists. Cohosted by Father Hardin and Sister Jane, the preparation for these shows was extensive. For example, a show that aired on October 31, 1975, contained an examination of the treatment of the topic of emancipation in the leading history textbooks used in Indiana schools. A show on August 9, 1983, featured an interview with Indianapolis mayor William Hudnut III, touching on a range of topics, such as housing, poverty, and crime in Indianapolis. In genial but assertive style, both Sister Jane and Father Hardin critiqued existing racism in government, education, and society as a whole. They emphasized the achievements of black professionals in Indiana, including artists, physicians, musicians, actors, and athletes. Several shows presented biographies of such figures as Sumner Furniss, the Bagby Brothers, Doctor George Washington Buckner, and the Ben Ishmaelites.[39]

The *Afro-American Journal* began as a monthly in February 1973, changed to a bimonthly publication in May/June, 1974, and later, in 1976, to a quarterly, finally ceasing publication in 1978. Father Hardin said that the schedule at the end was "whenever we could find the money."[40] The *Afro-American Journal* was a substantial newspaper-sized publication of ten to twenty pages, delivered to homes throughout the black community. Each issue featured a column by Father Hardin, who commented on current events; advocated for nonviolence, education, family values, or other approaches to problems in the black community; or documented key moments in the history of black people in Indianapolis. The journal contained scholarly articles on African and African American history by contributing experts at universities, poetry by local poets, reprints of historical documents or photos illustrating African or African American heritage, news about the Center, essays on various topics such as the black female, and even recipes and children's stories and puzzles. Sister Jane contributed heavily with background research and editing.

As the external voice for the Afro-American Institute, the *Afro-American Journal* mirrored the purpose of the institute in promoting education about the history and achievements of black Americans. Set in the context of the Black Power Movement of the late 1960s and early 1970s,[41] a time when black athletes raised their fists in a Black Power salute on the Olympics podium and the television miniseries *Roots* drew the attention of the country to the horrors of slavery, the journal echoed the themes of pride in black cultural achievements and African roots, indignation with the history of slavery and oppression, and the importance of education on political, social, and economic forces affecting black people. The journal printed stories of African historical luminaries and modern African nations to foster knowledge, pride, and reverence for the motherland; it included features on current crises and lifestyles to raise awareness and cultivate power. Whether disputing the notion of the "docile slave" or printing a recipe for banana fritters, the journal aimed to be an educational vehicle that would serve a wide range of interests.

Father Hardin as "radical priest" in Indianapolis, around 1970.

Father Hardin's column in the *Afro-American Journal* provided a record of his thinking during these turbulent years. He repeatedly expressed the purpose of the Afro-American Institute and the spirit of the times: "If the Black man is to be free, he must find the freedom within the knowledge of himself in his origin, destiny, culture, language, and the determination to share in this land which is his."[42] He discussed desegregation, nonviolence, black-on-black crime, consumerism, racism within the Catholic Church, and the need to support those living in poverty in Africa and in the United States. His language was often angry and skeptical of the sincerity of those in power. Sometimes, he used the slang of the time, such as fighting "THE MAN," or advising the establishment to "bug off." Throughout all his columns, historical pieces, and poetry, however, Father Hardin continued to preach the message of liberation through knowledge and informed action.

The two television documentaries produced by WRTV were written and narrated by Father Hardin. Sister Jane and Martin Center staff member Lois Kennedy were listed as history researchers.[43] In *For the Love of Freedom* (1976), Father Hardin appeared in African regalia at the Roberts Settlement, a pioneer farm community begun in 1835 north of Indianapolis by free men of mixed race who migrated from North Carolina to distance themselves from growing conflicts over slavery in the South. Father Hardin's narration detailed the history of the "Kingdom Builders," leaders of African tribes who brought prosperity and cultural achievements to their lands. He then traced the history of slavery and brought to light the ways in which the Catholic missionaries and early U.S. presidents engaged in the slave trade. Father Hardin concluded with the history of the modern "Kingdom Builders," the slaves who kept the dream of freedom alive and African Americans who made substantial contributions to Indiana.

In a second film, *The Kingdom Builders,* written and narrated by Father Hardin, he treated the history of Africa and slavery in greater depth than *For Love of Freedom*. The film focused on major American historical figures who owned slaves and it presented the Emancipation Act and Reconstruction through the insights of revisionist history. In the remainder of the film, Father Hardin talked about the effect of slavery on the economics and family structure of African Americans. He described early black inventors, Jim Crow laws and lynching, major African American abolitionist and cultural leaders, civil rights era events, and organizations such as the National Association for the Advancement of Colored People that arose to support equality. The film ends with Father Hardin's poem, "Freedom":

Alone with love and nowhere to take it
  Serving the earth and the people
Who walk upon it – FREEDOM

Together with others, waiting for an answer
    Jesus, Amen – I love you.
Thoroughly exhausted from hoping – FREEDOM

Fragrance of friendship, beckoning
    To all who can perceive
Untapped strength of peace
    Sighing – FREEDOM

Knowledge of God's face
    Man's ignominy and hunger
Touching the power of being – FREEDOM

Song in the night calls for
    Awakening
Let my people go – FREEDOM

Black-faced mammy tell Al
    Jolson about it, his back
Is too straight for a happy
    Slave – FREEDOM

Knowing my place, my people
    and my power
It's bound to come, maybe
    No other way but my own – FREEDOM

No one's going, it's coming
    We be, not alone
But with others, we be
    coming – FREEDOM

Stand up old folks, you
    young people act your age
And be respectful, watch us children
    For we be on our way – FREEDOM

The GLORY of the Black man is in
    no government's hands
Nor preacher's whine
    Nor can a dollar turn back time

If you don't pay no mind
>You'll miss us when we be

Coming by walking, walking . . .
>Heading for the promised land – FREEDOM[44]

The scholarship involved in these early efforts of the Center was extensive. Both Father Hardin and Sister Jane served as historians and researchers, spending long hours in libraries and archives. They made contact with others doing research on black history and culture, such as colleagues at the Smithsonian Institute. They traveled to sites such as the Frederick Douglass home to collect artifacts, photographs, and information. Gardner recalled spending long hours at libraries and preparing materials using the laborious techniques of the predigital period—manual typewriters and duplicating machines. Gardner described Sister Jane as a tireless researcher who worked in archives and libraries, gathering and classifying both scholarly and popular materials to provide intellectual content for workshops, programs, the journal, and exhibits.[45] Father Hardin and Sister Jane also enlisted contributions from top talent in the form of historians and archivists, writers and artists, as well as developing the talent of local assistants who had never before recognized or used their own talents in researching or depicting black history and culture.

Community reaction to the Center was mixed at first. While many in the black community participated eagerly and corporations lined up to educate their staffs about the new environment created by affirmative action, resentment bubbled over in some quarters. "The anxiety of alienating the Black community by associating with Whites and the fear of attracting the local Klan was ever present in the first years of Martin Center," Father Hardin recalled. "Bricks came through the windows, but we held on to our convictions: Nigra sum sedformasa [I am black, but beautiful. *Song of Songs,* 1:5.]"[46] Snooks Winger, Sister Jane's sister, recalled, "There was a time when [Father Hardin] actually feared for his life. . . . He came home from an evening meeting. Somebody had gotten into his home and they had stacked all his furniture in one pile, in a big heap, floor to ceiling. And I don't know if they had ever left signs or what . . . but he had been threatened. So it had to have been a terribly scary time."[47]

Sister Jane talked about receiving threats in the mail and on the phone and having to install security alarms in her living space, but she also talked about the confidence she drew from her association with Father Hardin: "Father Boniface was strong as a horse, you know. He just charged right on to everything. He taught me a lot about if you're scared, you're not going to do what you want to do, and you can't be scared of anything. And he taught me not to be scared."[48] She related how Father Hardin used prayer in difficult circumstances. At the end of each day, he would check on her safety by phone, ending with, "Go to bed and be at peace with God."[49] Also portraying Father Hardin as one who allayed anxieties and inspired courage, teacher and school administrator Payne said that he had "A lack of fear because he stood for truth and honesty and whatever it took, you know, when we saw him we knew, this has got to be the right cause that we're here for because he stood for that to us in the community . . . because he stood for truth, he had no fear."[50]

A document summarizing the accomplishments of the Center during its first three years of operation lists an impressive array of programs and number of participants.[51] A total of 62,919 people were reached through the center's programs, including intensive training, seminars for agencies, seminars for supervisors in industry and educational institutions, workshops, lectures, exhibits, puppet shows, consultation, and radio and television exposure. Gardner remembered the pace of these early years and the press for expansion. She portrayed the Center as a place where volunteers and part-time paid

INDIANAPOLIS RECORDER COLLECTION, INDIANA HISTORICAL SOCIETY

Father Hardin (center) collaborated closely with black ministers such as Reverend Benjamin Davis (left) and Reverend Andrew J. Brown (right), shown here attending the funeral of civic leader Lionel Artis in 1971.

staff learned as they went along, where staff worked with great enthusiasm as they discovered and shared new information on black heritage.[52]

Additional successes began to accumulate for the Center. Father Hardin was recognized with the first of what were to become regular awards, nominations, and designations in the community. Between 1970 and 1973, he was honored by the Citizens for Progress Committee, the Guys and Dolls organization, and the Associated Clubs. He received the Omega Citizen of the Year Award and the Martin Luther King Medal of Freedom, and he was asked to join the planning committee for the first Black Expo, an important community-service organization in Indianapolis that each year offers a noted Summer Celebration and the Circle City Classic football game.

The Sickle Cell Center's work was recognized as the model for other similar organizations, chiefly because it coupled genetic testing, education, and research. Although it began with strong collaboration with the Indiana University School of Medicine, the two became rivals in subsequent grant competitions as IU and the Martin Center engaged in a struggle to control the direction and resources of the Sickle Cell Center. The Sickle Cell Center's strong reputation and early successes helped to establish its independence from

MARTIN CENTER SICKLE CELL INITIATIVE PHOTO

Father Hardin and Doctor Raymond Pierce, director of the Sickle Cell Initiative of Martin Center.

Father Hardin explains Martin Center to Donna Pinckney and Biernette Burton at an NCAAP meeting in March 1974.

the School of Medicine and favored it in the competition for federal funds, a situation that caused some resentment.[53] As the need for newborn screening for sickle-cell disease became more generally acknowledged, the state of Indiana was the first to implement routine newborn screening. The decrease in newborn screening at the Sickle Cell Center enabled an increased focus on its educational mission. Father Hardin and Sister Jane maintained active roles as board members throughout the history of the Sickle Cell Center and had strong ideas about its operation. Doctor Pat Treadwell, president and member of the board of directors of the Sickle Cell Center, recalled Father's opposition to ending the screening, despite its financial costs.[54] He felt that control of the operation should be within the black community. Both he and Sister Jane were awarded commendations from the Sickle Cell Center.

As Father Hardin and Sister Jane surveyed the impact of the Martin Center's programs, they became convinced that the lack of education was holding back many in the black community. They began to dream of founding a school. One early concern was language. Those without standard written and oral expression were unable to compete for good jobs or argue their cause in interactions with the existing power structure. Father Hardin, quite accomplished as a linguist with varying degrees of competence in a reported fifteen or so languages, was especially sensitive to language. Therefore, early conceptualizations of what would eventually be Martin College focused on language.

Father Hardin described a second conceptualization in an interview to a reporter from the leading newspaper in the African American community, the *Indianapolis Recorder*. His intention was to develop, as a project of the Institute for African American Studies, an accredited alternative school that would serve both gifted and remedial students. "It will develop a student's talents in fields he is interested in or shows signs of deficiency," he said. "If a student is interested in the sciences or learning a foreign language, he is placed in accelerated classes to help him learn more about the subject. Whenever one of the students has trouble with reading or mathematics, he will be in a class to learn the subject at his own pace." He predicted the school would open in 1976.[55]

As Father Hardin and Sister Jane pondered their next steps, they focused on the need for educational credentials, specifically a higher-education degree, as the ticket to success. As Sister Jane noted, "Everything we ever did ended up with education."[56] They saw that underemployment locked people into low-paying jobs without hope of advancement. They realized that finances, poor experiences in a traditional college, poor prior schooling or achievement, jobs with rotating shifts or unpredictable overtime, parenting responsibilities, transportation problems, physical disabilities, and age all combined to discourage attendance at the existing institutions of higher education. They hoped, too, that educating parents would promote educational achievement in their children.

With typical confidence and disregard for the complexities entailed, Father Hardin decided to start a college. Sister Jane recalled their reasoning, "You'll never get ahead if you don't have a better education, so you can get a better job, because people can turn you away, just on that, [they'd say] 'well you don't have, you haven't even finished college. You can't have a job over there.' So he [Father Hardin] said, 'Well, if you can't have a job because you can't go to college, let's go make a college.'"[57]

Father Hardin and Sister Jane's resolve to found a college provided direction for their greatest achievement, an institution that was to become, in time, Martin University.

Chapter 4

"People said I was crazy," Hardin admitted with a laugh. "Some probably still think that. A lot of Black people do not believe that other Black people can educate them. We've kicked that stereotype. We're [Martin University] in the ghetto, we're in a poor section, we didn't go out somewhere, and we're available. I saw the gap in the educational system for the poor and those who were older. They were being put upon shelves."[1]

Father Boniface Hardin's intention to create a college was met with much skepticism. "I didn't get a lot of support. God loves babies and fools," he recalled.[2] A 2004 book of Martin University accomplishments observed, "The development of a college with the leadership by an African American man was received by the community with a smirk because of the racism that existed in Indianapolis and this attitude was adopted by some African Americans also. Support was negligible from all sides."[3] Yet, Father Hardin was hurt most deeply by the lack of support from the black community: "So if you ask me, in my last dying moments, what was most difficult, it would be that my people did not believe. I expected that other people would not believe, but the most difficult was that my people did not believe."[4]

Some support came from within his religious community at Saint Meinrad Archabbey. "For them I was okay now because education is something they understood. But they didn't understand the fact that I had an afro and wore African apparel—and that was a dashiki," said Father Hardin. "They didn't understand that I wanted to be aligned with the movement. But education was something they understood, so that kind of made me an all right guy, even though they expected me to fail. The expectation of failure was a given."[5] He later called Martin "the miracle that couldn't."[6] Charles Blair, program evaluator for the Lilly Endowment at the time, commented, "I don't think anybody believed that he could do it. And in fact, I think I told him once that it probably was not a possibility—and I wasn't doing it as my role as a [Lilly Endowment] program officer—I was just talking to him as a friend. It just seemed implausible. You know, you're going to start a university? Well, maybe I want to drive in the Indianapolis 500. I mean, 'It's just not feasible, Father

Hardin'—which is what I told him. And of course, he didn't listen and I think everybody had that thought. But he was so tenacious and so persistent and he stuck to it."[7]

The college would be called Martin Center College and would be nested within the Martin Center organizational umbrella. A central concept for the school was Martin Luther King Jr.'s concept of the "beloved community": the goal was to "instill this guiding spirit into a new academic community where oppressed peoples can throw off the bondage of despair and illiteracy and become capable of securing personal desires and freely-given labors as full citizens."[8]

The first target population for this college was the adult who had not been able to attend college right out of high school or who had attended but had been unable to graduate. Sister Jane Shilling, who served as the founding vice president, voiced the rationale: "How can we tell parents that their kids should go to college, and the kids say, 'Well *you* didn't go.' You know how kids are? So we said 'Well, let's just jump over that, and let's just get the adults to go to college.'"[9] The idea was to establish an expectation for college completion in families for whom the notion of higher education had seemed unattainable. Educated parents would nurture the development of their children as students; these educated parents would have better jobs and be better equipped to provide the economic security needed for their children's advanced levels of schooling. All adults, parents or not, would benefit from a higher-education credential that would enable them to take positions in companies, government, and the nonprofit sector, thus influencing the future and opening access to others.[10]

The college was also geared toward students who had left other colleges and universities without obtaining a degree, either through life circumstances or alienation with the culture of the institution they were attending. Father Hardin described the scene for black students at Indiana colleges, "Around here, there was a revolving door syndrome for the young black student. The student would go in, quit, or maybe get sent out."[11] The invitation to these students earned Martin the nickname "the Second Chance School."[12] Colleague John Sherman commented on the students who benefited from Father's approach: "I think he felt that they had been passed by. I'm not sure he ever used those words but I think that was his decision that they had been discriminated against, they had been lacking in self-confidence, they didn't have money, so you throw those altogether and it's very difficult. And when people knew they would be very welcome and they wouldn't be sitting in a room with eighteen year olds or in a room with people who had a much higher income level or [in situations where] perhaps they would be the only black person in the room or something, this was a sense of comfort that they could do that. So he knew these people had the capabilities but that they just had not had the opportunities so he provided those for people and . . . there was enormous gratitude for that."[13]

Steps toward the founding of a college proceeded incrementally. With a full program of workshops and educational programs already established, the leap to academic classes at the Martin Center was supported by these past curriculum efforts. Shortly after the founding of the center's Afro-American Institute in 1972, black studies courses were offered in cooperation with the local state university, Indiana University–Purdue University Indianapolis. Graduate credit through IUPUI was awarded for those who completed the courses, which were scheduled in intensive, rather than semester-long, offerings.[14]

In 1976 the Martin Center and IUPUI, under the guidance of IUPUI's Dean of the Faculty Jack Buhner, obtained a $100,000 Title I grant from the Indiana Higher Education Commission to examine higher-education opportunities for minority students in Indianapolis and surrounding areas. The report documented the need for a flexible, accessible program for nontraditional students. At first, IUPUI supported the idea of operating an alternative program led by the Center within the IUPUI structure, but Father Hardin came to believe that an independent four-year liberal arts college with a very experimental format was best led solely by the Center.[15] Although collaborative by nature, his instincts and desire to break with traditional ways of educating led Father Hardin to establish an institution independent of other institutions of higher learning, independent of the Catholic Church, and rooted in the African American experience. Father Hardin went to Antioch College in Yellow Springs, Ohio, to consult with a leader in the Union for Experimenting Colleges and Universities, Doctor King Cheek. Cheek came to the Martin Center and with his assistance, Father Hardin and Sister Jane looked into a number of "university without walls" programs and other experimental college formats. Cheek encouraged them to start a new kind of college for adults.[16]

The first step was to officially establish the new college, to be called Martin Center College, with the state of Indiana. In 1972 Indiana had passed a state law controlling the proprietary schools that had sprung up in the 1960s and 1970s. Since a new liberal arts college had not been founded in Indiana since the 1940s, Martin's request was handled by the Indiana Commission for Post-secondary Proprietary Schools even though it was not a proprietary school. A later self-study report to the North Central Association in 1990 provided some narrative on these early days: "On August 9, 1977 Martin Center College was given the license to do business in Indiana in spite of being told the old story to minorities: 'You're not ready.' For three years the College jumped through hoops, completed a self-study for the state, and fended off various attempts to dilute its curriculum. At first the State asked MCC [Martin Center College] to give an associate degree ('You're not ready for a bachelor's'), and then it suggested giving a bachelor of arts of applied sciences with no major (a degree which didn't even exist in the state)."[17] Doctor John Sullivan from the Union of Experimenting Colleges and Universities argued the case for state accreditation and was finally successful in 1979.

During this early period, Father Hardin and Sister Jane worked hard to develop the vision for the school, realizing that a traditional approach to teaching and learning was not appropriate for the students they were serving. They focused on the life experiences of the students, respected their time commitments and constraints, and provided a healing environment. They knew that the students they were to teach had not had success at existing colleges or had not even gained admission to them. A key concept that inspired Father Hardin and Sister Jane in formulating the Martin approach was that of andragogy, or teaching adult students. Andragogy is based on the idea, introduced by adult education scholar Malcolm Knowles,[18] that adult students bring a wealth of experience to the educational setting; therefore, dialogue and opportunities to reflect on and extend past learning are at the heart of the enterprise. Students are expected to play an important role in designing their learning experience and teachers are to function as guides and resources. Andragogical practices enacted at Martin included the use of discussion method over lecturing, arranging classroom seating in open squares or circles rather than rows, code-velopment of the syllabus by the adult educator and students, and creation of assignments that permitted students to actively explore new learning from the standpoint of their existing accomplishments.[19] While other institutions have since adopted elements of this approach, Martin was a pioneer in enacting it.

Father Hardin and Sister Jane's embracing of andragogy was closely aligned with the emancipatory character they wished to infuse in the new college. Inspired by Paulo Freire, whose *Pedagogy of the Oppressed* was a standard reading connected with educational activities and ideas at Martin, both administrators strived to create a "healing environment" in the new college. Along with Freire, they believed that their students had been oppressed by existing social structures and dominant actors, causing them to lose faith in themselves and their abilities. They knew that the oppressed need to take an active role in liberating themselves through shaping their education and that oppressor and oppressed had to be colearners in the process. The ethnotherapy approach used at Martin Center, a blend of small-group counseling and experiential learning, was adopted to help students process the ways in which they had been oppressed or had oppressed others over the course of their lifetimes. Reflective writing, drama, group projects, and other forms of learning were to be combined with powerful readings to create a nurturing and healing environment. Reflecting about this approach in 2001, Father Hardin said, "Learning is a mystical experience: physical and spiritual. Both learners, students and teachers, must be engaged in this experience. When an oppressed person arrives at the fountain of knowledge, wounds of life are brought there and the co-learners must be ready to share in the healing and learning experience. Students who struggle to overcome the difficulties of the head, heart, and hand, whether in ordinary life or in prison life, have an extraordinary capacity to philosophize, as in metaphysics, the ability to write essays, poetry and speeches. They reach an extraordinary level of success if responded to on a personal level; even more so in drama when given an opportunity to portray someone else who has struggled and overcome. The healing and liberation comes as a result of this environment, a process that requires understanding, wisdom, power and patience, individually and collectively."[20]

The new college honored life experience through the use of Assessment of Prior Learning, later called Prior Learning Assessment, a method for determining the match between students' past learning and academic content that would grant college credit for knowledge that students had upon entry. Father Hardin later described this concept: "The uniqueness of our school is that we have an assessment of prior learning. That means that you may have a year somewhere else at another college . . . but you may have worked for 5 years. So you worked in a business, or you ran your father's office and you're a manager and you learned a lot about debits and credits and so forth and you said, 'Hey, you know, I never finished my degree because I had to work for my father, but I really need that now, and I don't want to go back and get on a campus and go through all of that.' Well then we look through that 5 years of experience and we find out how much college level learning is there."[21] Father Hardin and

Sister Jane consulted with the Council for Advancement and Evaluation of Learning and adapted that organization's model to the Martin framework.[22] At its origins, Martin was the only black college to offer assessment of prior learning and one of the few colleges nationally to do so.

Finally, flexibility had to be a hallmark of the new institution. Martin students often had to cope with "job responsibilities such as rotating shifts or unpredictable overtime, parenting responsibilities, age, failure in another institution (for reasons other than their ability), transportation problems, or physical handicap."[23] Martin featured evening, intensive, and hybrid classes as important formats for combating scheduling issues; a holistic approach that valued health, family, and economic realities; and mentoring and the creation of a warm and accepting psychological environment for retaining students and ensuring their success. Clearly, a college based on principles of andra-gogy, emancipation, and student-centeredness was going to be a different enterprise. It was a model that required constant explanation to accreditation agencies and other regulators, funders, faculty, and students. Father Hardin and Sister Jane spent their days reading, talking with experts, and struggling to articulate their vision of the new college. Their excitement and focus added new energy to the Martin Center.

In 1992 Father Hardin summed up what he called the "education revolu-tion" inherent in the Martin approach: "Martin says that andragogy should be used with adults not pedagogy. Martin says that every institution must choose a positive, therapeutic and holistic learning environment and reject all the 'isms' that exclude, denigrate or hurt people. Martin says that a uni-versity must be a catalyst for change in a community, on the cutting edge of human need and service. Martin says that the *anawin Jahweh* [rejected of the Lord—poor, powerless people] must be offered excellence in *scienta et sapientia* [knowledge and wisdom], respect and honor; standard learning and teaching must not be tolerated."[24]

In 1980 the North Central Association of Colleges and Schools' Commis-sion on Institutions of Higher Learning granted Martin candidacy for accredi-tation, which endowed the fledgling institution with new respect. Doctor Ted Hallenbeck from the Union for Experimenting Colleges and Universities had consulted with Father Hardin and Sister Jane for three years in preparation for this step. The US Department of Health, Education, and Welfare followed suit immediately afterward and granted Martin eligibility to compete for federal grants and extend financial aid to its qualified students. Later in the same year,

Martin attained fully accredited status with the Indiana Commission for Post-secondary Education. Then, in order to receive the highly important national accreditation by the North Central Association of Colleges and Universities, the college had to issue two biennial reports and undergo both a focused evaluation and comprehensive review for full accreditation. Sister Jane played a key role in learning the standards of the North Central Association, making sure that Martin met them, and documenting the ways in which the college was worthy of accreditation. Her research and writing ability, as well as her leadership as an educator, were central to the success of the accreditation efforts.

Martin opened in 1977 with only a few students, five or seven depending on the source.[25] One report implied that these students were from the CETA (Comprehensive Employment and Training Act) program at the Center.[26] An unusual characteristic of these first students is that they were white. Father Hardin later recalled, "I didn't know how that was going to work out, you know, because I got a little nervous. But then it started to turn."[27] The college was housed at 3559 and 3553 North College Avenue, just north of the other Martin Center buildings. A large portrait of Mary McLeod Bethune, the founder of Bethune-Cookman University, graced the entrance hallway, likely as an inspiration to Father Hardin and Sister Jane. The Indianapolis Foundation provided capital support of $250,000 for the new college. Adjunct faculty were recruited through newspaper classifieds for specific courses and paid $150 per course; Father Hardin and Sister Jane were the administrators and full-time faculty. Most teaching was one-on-one. Students learned in homes as well as at the Martin building. One of the first students, Norris Milton Archer, remembered how informal the learning settings were. "One of my instructors came to the house and we ponder[ed] over characters such as Malcolm X and the little Haitian General Toussaint, Frederick Douglass and more. On one occasion I studied Psychology with Maureen Prevost at her home near Butler University. Several others conducted my studies at their place of business."[28]

By the following year, thirty students were enrolled and Martin began to use a classroom setup in which students were facing each other in the open square that became the normal andragogical arrangement. In 1978 a registrar was hired, and in 1979 a dean responsible for the Assessment of Prior Learning program was hired.[29] That same year, Martin College was established as a separate corporation from the Martin Center, but was assisted by the Center in meeting its financial operations until 1985.[30]

By 1980 there were 150 students enrolled and Father Hardin received grant-writing help to apply to the Lilly Endowment for funding for enrollment and operations. Although this was before the school was officially accredited, Father Hardin convinced Doctor William Bonefield, vice president of education at the Lilly Endowment, that the candidacy status recently granted by the

MARTIN UNIVERSITY

The original Martin Center College location, 3553 North College Avenue, Indianapolis.

North Central Association meant that Martin was ready for accreditation. The college received its initial grant of $50,000 and with that, a history of support from the Lilly Endowment began. Traditionally, this foundation directed its resources toward education, religion, and the arts, and favored local institutions in Indiana. Once he had been recognized as a serious educator in the early years of the Martin Center, Father Hardin established a warm relationship with program directors and officers that stood him well in seeking funds over the years. These included Charles Blair, Willis Bright, Ralph Lundgren, and Sara Cobb.

At this juncture, Father Hardin was nearing fifty and made adjustments in his approach to change and to community powerbrokers. He looked back on his earlier years of activism that had been characterized by the anger of youth and realized that more positive methods were needed. "I began to realize that anger is a self-aggrandizing experience," he said. "We had to find other ways to deal with our indignity because anger just led to more anger." He turned to the Rule of Saint Benedict and its foundation of contemplation, prayer, and reflection on Scripture to find a new way.[31] Blair described this change, "He knew that to be a servant of the people that he chose to serve, he could not let his ego get in the way of that. I think that when you're a young man . . . you tend to be a little impetuous and you tend to be a little more ego driven and as you get a little bit older and you want to help people and you really want to serve people, you've got to put that aside and that's what I saw him do. So he asked people for help whom he formerly had had an adversarial relationship with, that included the city, the city of Indianapolis, the mayor. . . . Over time, he went back to some of those same people in a more humble fashion and began to say, 'Look, I'm trying to do something that will help. And will you help me, even though in the past we may have had problems but will you help me now? I'm doing something worthwhile.' And over time, people started to wear down because he kept asking. He wouldn't stop."[32]

In 1981 Martin celebrated the graduation of its first student, James Griffey, who received a bachelor of arts in management and accounting. Four more students graduated in 1982, one of whom, Archer, an Indianapolis city administrator, had a private ceremony in the office of Mayor William Hudnut before group graduations were held at Saint Peter Claver Center. Six students graduated in 1983, sixteen in 1984, and twenty-three in 1985.[33] Tuition was $250 per course in 1984–85.[34] By 1988 Martin had graduated 140 students. Most of the degrees awarded were in various business and health and human service areas.[35] Martin became a member of the Consortium for Urban Education, a group of colleges in the Indianapolis area, as well as the Independent Colleges of Indiana. Doctor Lou Gatto, then president of Marian College, another Indianapolis institution, paved the way for membership and even paid the membership fee.[36] The support and welcoming stance of other area higher-education institutions was very important to Martin: Father Hardin cultivated these relationships through regular visits and phone calls to key administrators at these schools. From the start in 1977, IUPUI made a major contribution, allowing Martin students official access to its library, an arrangement that continues.

The year 1987 was a banner one in the history of Martin. The North Central Association of Colleges and Schools had granted the all-important full accreditation on February 24 without reservation. Father Hardin and Sister Jane were bursting with pride that this step had been achieved on the first try. The enormous amount of time they had spent in providing documentation to the organization finally reaped the reward. Former faculty member Liz Staton recalled that to celebrate the accreditation success, Father Hardin gathered up nine cars and transported the faculty and staff to Saint Meinrad Archabbey, where he had been a student, seminarian, and assistant treasurer. He was euphoric to have achieved this milestone and wanted those involved to have a day off to celebrate by scheduling a tour and picnic.[37]

Also in 1987 a new prospect for expanding the physical campus emerged. Although the board of trustees had looked into purchasing a larger building as early as 1984,[38] possible funding through community block grants or other sources had failed to materialize. In 1987 Robert Kolentus, a faculty member then serving as registrar, drew Father Hardin's attention to property owned by the Archdiocese of Indianapolis in the Martindale-Brightwood neighborhood. The site was the former Saint Francis de Sales Catholic Church and School, once a thriving parish of more than 3,000 members; by 1987 the neighborhood was experiencing a downturn in population caused by the physical barrier created by the construction of Interstate 70 just south of the parish and the exodus of its middle-class families as the railroad and business employers in the area relocated. When the parish numbered fewer than 300, the archdiocese closed it and its buildings sat empty.

The property included a church, a rectory, a convent, a school, and several residential houses, as well as parking lots and vacant lots. Father Hardin approached the archbishop about the sale. As Kolentus told the story, the bishop asked Father how much he could offer. When Father suggested $100, the archbishop asked him to raise that amount to $1,000 to at least cover the cost of preparation of deeds and other legal documents. Kolentus estimated that the actual worth of the property was about $4.5 million, although the official

The Martin University Peace Garden.

MARTIN UNIVERSITY

purchase price had been reduced to $300,000 as the years passed without a buyer and the neighborhood continued to deteriorate.[39] Former Martin trustee Tom McKenna suggested that the willingness of the archdiocese to enable this transaction might have reflected the guilt that it bore for its past treatment of Father Hardin. It also established a way for both the archdiocese and Saint Meinrad to support him at arms' length by giving him a separate space in which to do his work.[40] Kolentus postulated that the deal was an incident of divine intervention. He observed "God has always worked with this school," illustrating his point with the story of how Father and Sister were once paying bills and came up $20,000 short. They opened the last envelope on the desk and found, instead of one more bill, a $20,000 contribution. "So, God has taken care of this place; it's always been a place of faith, very much so," said Kolentus.[41]

Sister Jane told the amusing story of how she and Father Hardin first went to look at the Saint Francis de Sales property to see if it would be suitable. They opened the door to one building and found that the leaking roof had destroyed much of the interior; there were large icicles hanging from the rafters, where pigeons were roosting. The floor was covered in pigeon droppings and other debris. Sister reported being aghast until Father turned to her with stars in his eyes. "Janey," he said, "This is great!"[42] That kind of vision led to the gradual shift from the College Avenue campus to the new location, called the Avondale campus, since it was based along Avondale Place south of East Twenty-Second Street. At the celebration of accreditation and the dedication of the Saint Francis de Sales site, notables such as former U.S. vice president Dan Quayle, Indiana governor Robert Orr, and Indianapolis mayor Hudnut attended.[43]

During the 1987–88 school year, students attended classes at both locations, but gradually offices and classes were moved to the Avondale campus as the properties were renovated. Father Hardin bought up neighborhood homes as they went up for sale, often at very depressed prices. Some homes were demolished for parking lots and eventually for new construction. At first, faculty offices were in the former rectory. The church was used as a fine-arts center and site of larger gatherings, such as the first on-campus graduation in 1987 (previous graduations had been held in various community facilities). The former elementary school was devoted to classrooms and student resource centers. Needed renovations for converting from elementary school to college use included replacing small fixtures in the bathrooms and obtaining adult-size furniture. Fortunately, Purdue University donated used tables and chairs.[44] Alumna Mynelle Gardner recalled the student experience with the facilities: "All of us old timers joke about the building because we said at the time you had to know where to sit in class in order not to get rained on. When it rained they had a leaky roof because they didn't get the money to fix the roof. It was patch, patch, patch. And so we said, you had to. But that didn't stop anyone because it seemed like—you understood that. You wanted what it had to give, you knew what it had to give."[45]

At first Father Hardin stayed in his office on College Avenue, but eventually moved to a university-owned house on Avondale Place, just across the street from the church, rectory, and school. He recalled that it was refreshing to hear the sounds of the nearby railroad rather than the police sirens of College Avenue.[46] Priscilla Dillon, who served in the university's development office, described Father's office: "The house was quite crowded. It was a room probably about 12 feet by 14 feet maybe and bookcases with lots of books in them. And he had this high backed chair and his desk and then at one end was a small conference table. He enjoyed astronomy and in the house he would

Father Hardin working outside his first "office" in a small house at the new Avondale campus.

FATHER BONIFACE HARDIN COLLECTION, INDIANA HISTORICAL SOCIETY

put—because he ran out of space of where to hang pictures—so he put them on the ceiling. So it was fun to go there and see what picture he added to the ceiling."[47] She recalled that Father often conducted transactions while sitting on the front steps of the house. Approachability and informality were hallmarks of his style. "And then he would walk," Dillon recalled. "Sometimes he would say, 'Come walk with me.' And we would [walk] around campus and I think that was his way of getting some exercise too and maybe working off some stress."[48]

Martin developed and implemented the practice of andragogy—adult-oriented teaching—throughout its educational programs. Knowles continued his assistance after his retirement, making several trips to the campus to consult and to conduct workshops over the next several years, charging only expenses. Knowles later demonstrated his enthusiasm for what Martin was doing by becoming a donor.[49]

In 1988 Martin established yet another campus, this one called Lady Elizabeth College, at the Indiana Women's Prison. The campus, named after Father Hardin's mother, Elizabeth, offered bachelor's degrees to expand on a program of course offerings originally developed by Ball State University. It was an example, Father Hardin said, of Martin's mission to "the total community."[50] Over the years, Lady Elizabeth College graduated twenty-four students, which sometimes caused resentment among those in the Indianapolis community who argued that prisoners should not have such privileges. A newspaper story and supportive editorial that profiled graduate Paula Cooper, a convicted murderer who had been imprisoned since the age of sixteen, drew irate letters from community members who resented any way in which taxpayers were supporting prisoner education.[51] (A subsequent letter writer detailed that private funds and loans were used.)[52] Even when the federal government ended loans to prisoners in 1995, Martin University continued to teach students at Lady Elizabeth, accepting only available state funds. This arrangement continued until the inmates were moved to Rockville Prison in 2003.

Father Hardin's education at Saint Meinrad inculcated great respect for the liberal arts. He often spoke of the importance of the trivium (grammar, logic, and rhetoric) and the quadrivium (arithmetic, geometry, music, and astronomy), which are the seven disciplines that composed the liberal arts from the sixth century through medieval times. He frequently referenced the great, but little discussed, history of achievement in the liberal arts by such black scholars as W. E. B. Du Bois.[53] His intent was to root the Martin educational experience in the liberal arts; he saw these as the foundation for wisdom that would enable graduates to live full lives of service. Although not opposed to majors that would lead directly to careers, Father Hardin and Sister Jane insisted on a strong liberal arts core. The initial Martin catalog in 1987 listed twelve majors: accounting, counseling, biology, communications, social problems management, drama, history, public administration, marketing administration, psychology, sociology, and English. Over the course of Father Hardin's and Sister Jane's tenure, the number of majors ebbed and flowed between twenty and twenty-six undergraduate majors, with such programs as African-American studies, business administration, computer technology, early childhood education, fine arts/music, marketing, genetic counseling, mathematics, music, political science, religious studies, and criminal justice as consistent majors, and such applied majors as addictions counseling, insurance, environmental science, and human resources management appearing for periods of time. Psychology and various forms of counseling were particularly strong areas for Martin; the addition of master's programs in community psychology and urban ministry strengthened these areas. One signature program, genetic counseling, stemmed from the work of the Martin Center's Sickle Cell program, and was unique for its time.

Father Hardin and Sister Jane were always careful to develop only those

Sister Jane Edward Schilling, Vice President of Martin University, circa 2000.

programs that were consistent with community needs and goals. The Institute of Urban Ministry Studies arose from the deliberations of a focus group and advisory council comprised of approximately sixteen to eighteen ministers and lay persons from churches in the Indianapolis black community. Having conducted a Lilly Endowment-sponsored nine-month study in 1989–90 of the educational background of ministers and other leaders of 200 area churches, the council found that only one-third of the respondents had finished high school and fewer than one-fifth of the pastors were college graduates. Moved by the desire on the part of the ministers for a program that would extend their education, Martin developed a degree proposal for a degree in urban ministry studies that was approved by the Higher Learning Commission in 1990.[54]

A second graduate degree emerged from the same study, which documented the need for an educational program in pastoral care and counseling. The North Central Association team recommended a degree in community psychology as a better fit. Father Hardin and Sister Jane worked to develop the graduate faculty for this program, which Martin eventually divided into two tracks, counseling psychology and organizational psychology and leadership.

Through the development of these two graduate programs, Martin successfully petitioned the Higher Learning Commission to change its name and status to Martin University in 1990. It was now approved to offer bachelor's degrees as well as two master's programs, one in urban ministry and the other in community psychology. Between 1990 and 2004, initial graduate enrollment grew from ten students to ninety-five.

Community members also requested that the university establish a teacher education program for both aspiring teachers and veteran teachers within the

Father Hardin, late 1990s.

MARTIN UNIVERSITY

area school systems who would increase the presence of teachers who were competent in dealing with the needs of poor, urban students. Buoyed by Father Hardin's belief that the teacher "is the most sacred person in the black community,"[55] Martin explored ways to establish such a program. Through a partnership with the University of Indianapolis, Martin at first worked with Indiana's AmeriCorps program to collaborate on a joint teacher education program, but the necessity for the students to take daytime classes at the University of Indianapolis prevented the program from being successful. Martin then undertook the effort to begin its own program. With assistance from Indiana University and its core campus in Indianapolis, IUPUI, Martin made preparations to achieve accreditation by the National Council for Accreditation of Teacher Education. (The process of seeking this approval was interrupted by the new leadership at Martin when Father Hardin and Sister Jane retired, but development was resumed in 2014.)[56]

Father Hardin's fondness for liberal learning and service to the community led to his emphasis on programs that would produce self-knowledge, wisdom, and leadership skills in graduates. In 1997 he established a program in humane exchange, which captured many of his goals for students. This bachelor's degree program explored "human interaction using transformative and liberating practices."[57] Students looked at human interaction in a variety of contexts using multiple disciplinary perspectives to prepare for work as change agents in human services who would focus on discriminatory attitudes and practices in order to advocate, mediate, and use prevention strategies. Father Hardin also envisioned a Centre for Humane Exchange, which was never realized, but was to be a large-scale effort focused on improving society and the environment.[58]

As the Avondale campus continued to increase its enrollment, Father Hardin began to envision expansion and construction of a new campus building, the first new building in Martin's history. Anticipating such an occurrence, he had been buying up properties surrounding the original church buildings. Colleague Marty Greenan recalls seeing early sketches of what became the

Father Hardin in special hard hat overseeing construction of the Martin University Education Center, the first new building for the university, 2000.

Education Center during visits with Father Hardin in the 1990s.[59] The ambitious president had already sketched a building with a globe, which became a major component of the finished building. Although possibilities for relocating Martin to larger facilities near the Indiana Fairgrounds had surfaced, Father

Father Hardin at window of Education Center, under construction in 2000.

MARTIN UNIVERSITY

Hardin was committed to the Martindale-Brightwood neighborhood and wanted Martin to be a central asset to that community.

With $5 million in funding from the Lilly Endowment, augmented by do-nations during a significant capital campaign in 1999–2000, and a bank loan of $2 million, the new building became a reality. In August 1999 Father Hardin organized a "planting" ceremony, during which staff and students planted various landscaping pieces to kick off the capital campaign by symbolizing the life and respect for nature that would surround the new building. Father Hardin took great interest in the architectural details, working with the staff of Schmidt Associates, an Indianapolis architectural firm. The new building would embody central ideas that he valued—a massive steel-and-glass globe on the front of the building to represent the inclusive nature of the scholar-ship at Martin and its reverence for the earth and connections to all peoples; the open space "Gathertorium," which exemplified the emphasis on commu-nity and avoidance of the one-way communication that the term "auditorium" conveys; the careful use of natural materials to show the value of conserva-tion; and a Peace Garden, with a stream that wandered through the campus to emphasize harmony and joy.

Adorned with a specially decorated hard hat, Father Hardin toured the construction site frequently, discussing progress with the workers and archi-tects. The glass for the globe was imported from England; 325 million-year-old sandstone quarried in Mansfield, Indiana, along with bricks and steel from In-diana were used on the walls; and black slate from Italy was imported for trim. The new building provided nine classrooms, administrative and faculty offices, space for reflection, the Gathertorium, and offices for various programs such as the smoking cessation program. Excitement was in the air as the new build-ing was dedicated in October of 2001. "This building and the people who touch it are the outward signs of the invisible grace and wisdom within—*scientia et sapientia osculatasunt*—knowledge and wisdom have kissed—theologically, this is called sacrament."[60]

From the initial five students enrolled at Martin, enrollment rose steadily. By 1980 the student count was approximately 105 students and stayed steady during the years prior to the move to the Avondale campus, after which there was space for the recruitment of more students. Between 1990 and 2000, enrollment grew to 500 students. The addition of the Yarbro program in 2002 to prepare traditional-age students from feeder high schools boosted total enrollment to more than 700 students by 2004. Enrollment during the last

MARTIN UNIVERSITY

The Martin University Education Center, opened in 2001.

year of Father Hardin's presidency, 2007–08, jumped to 961 students. By that time, 1,370 bachelor's and master's degrees had been awarded by Martin. The student body came to consist of primarily African American students, a large proportion of which were women, with an average student age hovering around thirty-eight.

Recruitment of students at Martin began with word-of-mouth efforts on the part of Father Hardin and Sister Jane. Father became known for approaching people without degrees as he traversed the community, urging them to come to Martin. Alumnus Clete Ladd told of being accosted by Father Hardin as he left a barbershop and then again some years later when he failed to enroll. Alumnus Mikal Saahir was approached by Father as he answered a fire-alarm call to Martin. He recalled, "He leaned toward me and said, 'You're the imam [meaning the leader of the mosque].' He said, 'You shouldn't be driving a fire truck.' He said, 'Come and talk with me, I'll see if I can get you into school.'"[61] Father Hardin not only gave these potential students personal tours and encouragement, but also checked to see that they were attending their first classes.[62] These two were not exceptional cases. Even though Martin eventually hired recruitment staff and formed an office of student enrollment, Father Hardin and Sister Jane continued to speak to people at bus stops, restaurants, and other everyday environments. Gardner described the process: "They would initiate a friendly conversation with the person, ask them about their goals in life, and take the occasion to encourage high expectations and confidence in the potential student. Boniface recruited students everywhere. We'd be in McDonald's and he would stop a worker and say, 'Do you have a college degree?' And we'd think, 'Oh no, here it goes.' Or, he would sit on the corner there when we had a place to sit on and he would talk with anyone who passed. He'd say, 'Are you going to school?' And the next thing you know, we'd be enrolling that person."[63]

These encounters usually ended with an invitation to come for a personal tour of Martin. Father frequently conducted these visits by prospective students himself. Father and Sister were well-known in the community and relied on contacts with families and friends to spread the word about Martin. A list of venues for Martin recruitment demonstrates the grassroots nature of finding students: correctional institutions, beauty shops, day-care centers, malls, laundromats, bowling alleys, check cashing offices, and shelters.[64]

One special program that combined recruitment and community service goals was the Indiana College Preparatory Program for K–12 students, funded by the Lilly Endowment. This program provided educational services, ranging from tutoring to archeology activities to music lessons for children from three nearby neighborhoods. The goal was to expose children to enrichment activities within a university environment, in the hope that both parents and children would pursue higher education, ideally at Martin University.[65]

Faculty and staff were recruited locally for the most part. Following the early days when part-timers were hired through newspaper classifieds and paid $150 a course, Martin later began to employ full-time faculty and hired adjuncts to teach in specialty areas. Continual staff development, primarily led by Sister Jane, was needed to imbue the Martin philosophies of teaching in faculty, especially adjuncts, who were not at the school full time. Finding specialists who also bought into the practices of andragogy and ethnotherapy and embraced the needs of the largely nontraditional African American student body was challenging. Greenan recalled that Sister Jane summarily dismissed three nuns who had been recruited for teaching posts when she learned that they were teaching in traditional ways and would not respond to instructions to adopt an andragogical approach.[66] Father Hardin sometimes cultivated those with specific knowledge bases, such as genetics or early child education, to pursue advanced degrees so that they might eventually teach at Martin.

Staff members often came from among alumni ranks. In 2004 Martin graduates made up 39 percent of the staff. The university's philosophy stated: "While most colleges and universities worry that when carried to excess this practice encourages 'in-breeding and insular thinking,' the Martin experience thus far seems to suggest that it builds quality and pride."[67] Father also found places for people in need on the staff, a practice that was challenged by some and admired by others. While Sister and others sometimes found fault with the practice of hiring underqualified people who had appealed to Father for a job, the many success stories of people rising to the situation and becoming loyal and energetic professionals affirmed Father's belief in the untapped potential of many in the community. Father's compassion paid off more often than not.

Faculty and staff loyalty were paramount at Martin. At times Father Hardin had to ask them to make the ultimate sacrifice—postponement or reduction of wages due to cash shortfalls or cash-flow problems. During these periods, he told faculty and staff that they could take a salary reduction or postponement or leave with a good recommendation. Repeatedly, almost every member chose to stay and often, each received restitutions and eventual pay increases. In a few instances, Father Hardin had to make personnel cuts. He spoke of one such instance when he worried about the impact on families of his employees, "There was not enough enrollment this summer, so we had to reduce the staff across the board. I nearly died when I had to tell them—it hurt a lot."[68]

Former students depict a learning environment that was warm and nurturing. Most used the phrase "like a family" to describe the school, singling out the environment as profoundly different from the one they encountered at other institutions. Brenda Shaheed, who had been to two different colleges before attending Martin, attained both her bachelor's and master's degrees and became an administrator at Martin. She reflected on her experience, "So many times we've been told that we weren't college material. We didn't have what it took to be successful. And for me to be able to share with people as we would bring them in, 'You can do this,' to see the fear and the anxiety of individuals thinking, 'Oh, I don't know whether I can do this because I've been told I'm not college material, I'm not smart enough.' But then to see the end of that at graduation and the jubilation of their families. Oh, it was miraculous, it was just beautiful, it was just beautiful." Graduates, Shaheed said, would say to their Martin mentors, "'No one ever talked to me, no one ever talked to me the way you talked to me. No one ever showed me that they cared the way you care about me.' That's what made it so special."[69]

Former students repeatedly cited one course, emancipatory narratives, for its profound effect on their thinking. In a newspaper interview Father Hardin described the motivation behind the class: "The healing comes from the classroom, where students talk about themselves. . . . It gives the student a chance to really tell their stories. You have to be about the business of dealing with yourself and healing yourself."[70] Narratives of prominent people in history who had triumphed over oppression or promoted ways for others to find freedom constituted the main readings for the class, but the culmination was the writing of one's own narrative. Ladd described the power of the class: "That course peels off the layers of not only historical prejudices but your own prejudices. And as people start sharing their own experiences, then, you also see how you've been prejudiced or discriminated against others, that it is a two-way street. We started off talking about some of the things in history: slavery, AMAFA, holocaust, Native American things, and then how we get into blaming people and then we become victims and never get out of being victimized, we never get out of the sense of we're still victims."[71]

Gardner recalled that Father Hardin often brought in props to stimulate discussion. One evening he displayed a model of a clipper ship and asked students what associations they had with the ship. Gardner described her reaction: "And he said, 'Okay, tell me, what does this mean to you?' And people were talking about, you know, on the ocean, and all this and all of that. And I remember one young man. I was thinking it, but he said it before I could get it out. He said, 'To me it's a slave ship.' And that's when Father started his dialogue about how things have different meanings to people. You have to understand this. Because this ship didn't mean the same thing to me as to the whites in the class."[72] Students were alternately affirmed and surprised as Father empathized with the ways in which they were hurt, but broadened their understanding of oppression. Ladd was stunned to learn that one of the first slaves sold in the United States was an Irish woman.[73] In keeping with his ethnotherapeutic approach, Father Hardin aimed to help students identify and deal not only with the ways they were oppressed, but also to understand how they and others were oppressors of social groups other than their own. In their final narratives for the course, students wrote about the journey into their self-understanding and the liberation and empowerment they experienced. The course was, and still remains, a requirement for all majors, a cornerstone of the Martin experience, which aimed to heal and educate broadly for civic and societal improvement as well as to enhance career success.

All students at Martin had to do a final thesis that integrated and enhanced their studies. Many of these projects were full-fledged studies of local problems, history, or biographies. Saahir's project led to the publication of two books, one a biography of the Honorable Elijah Muhammad, and the other a children's book titled *By Winter and Summer*. Father Hardin's respect for Saahir's Muslim tradition led him to encourage this extended exploration. Father Hardin and Sister Jane took great care to elicit students' interests in formulating a plan for the final project. One of Father's favorite questions was "What is your purpose in life?" a question so fundamental that it forced a focus on essentials and a sometimes uncomfortable examination of past experiences and self-image. Ladd described how his thesis topic was decided. In conversation with Father Hardin, he lamented that he, like many other black males, did not have a father figure to help guide them through life transitions. As a National Guard journalist assigned to cover the Mojave Desert, he wrote a story about Native Americans who took their sons through an initiation ritual called Vision Quest. He became fascinated with the idea of rite of passage and compared it to his own life experience. Ladd said, "If I had something like that in my childhood ushering me into adulthood, I think myself and others, particularly inner city males, would have a better concept of becoming men, responsible men citizens, things of that nature, before crime, teen parenthood, those kinds of things. Because [without such an experience] we would see ourselves as men by how well we could fight, get women or girls, how much we could drink or smoke, but with this Native American culture it was more about becoming a member of your community. And we didn't have that. And I was talking to Father about this, and he said, 'That's your thesis.' And I was like, wow, okay. He had that way of bringing things out of you."[74] Father Hardin then provided him with resources about rites of initiation in other cultures and religions that enabled him to research the thesis. Students also composed portfolios of work that summed up their prior learning and academic experiences at Martin University.

Father Hardin was a familiar presence in the halls of the university. He often sat in on classes or engaged students in conversations in the hallways. Former student Margaret Smith recalled how Father Hardin educated through simple conversation: "You could just go in his office and you'd come out shaking your head. . . . 'Well, I didn't know that.' You could see him in the hall at school . . . and you could talk with him for ten minutes and you'd say, 'Well, I didn't know that.'"[75] Ladd reported that Father Hardin peeked in his classroom

MARTIN UNIVERSITY

Father Hardin, circa 2000. This image was made into a commemorative postage stamp.

on his first day to make sure that he really came to class. Ladd said, "And the thing about it is he made me feel special, he made me feel like I was almost the only student there. And I did feel that way, but after talking with other people, he made everybody feel like they were the only student there. I think that was one of his gifts, to make you feel you were someone unique, and that he cared about you as an individual."[76] (Ladd's relationship with Father Hardin developed to the extent that he was comfortable calling him "Father," the first time in his life that he was able to use that term.) Instructors reported that this concern was universal. For example, they and Father Hardin often provided students with a few dollars for transportation so that they could get to or from school and home.

Sister Jane met with students to discuss academic progress. Her manner was often more pointed and probing, challenging students to clarify their ideas or improve their writing. At the basis of her critical stance, however, was a deep concern for students, which she manifested in many ways. Aware that many students were coming to Martin directly from their day jobs, she made large pots of soup to sustain them for the evening classes and greeted students as they entered. She came to know each student individually, and the highlight of graduation was Sister Jane's tribute to each student, in which she recounted challenges the student had to face, their main interests, and their achievements. Even as the number of graduates increased, the tradition continued and Martin graduations were a joyous celebration of triumph over adversity. By the time Father and Sister retired in 2007, Martin had awarded 1,360 bachelor's and master's degrees. Father delighted in citing statistics about how many graduates had gone on to do additional graduate work and how many had taken on such important roles as deputy mayor or fire chief in the city.

To Father Hardin, all members of the Martin community had to be united in a special way. He said, "In this institution, which is nondenominational, we try to teach each other—the students, the faculty, the staff, that they ought to love each other. Now all the knowledge in the world and you don't have love and care for each other [is not what we are about]. Because you can take knowledge and hurt people.—But true love can't hurt anybody."[77] In hiring decisions, in curriculum design, and in the ways in which business was conducted at Martin, love was a central principle.

Father Hardin made it clear that Martin University was not a Catholic school. He said, "My Catholicity is personal, it's personal."[78] Yet although Martin University was founded as a private, nonsectarian institution, spirituality permeated its operations. Prayers were offered at the beginnings of meetings, public assemblies, meal functions, and on major occasions. Father Hardin was careful to use the names for the deity favored by the world's major religions in serial fashion—Allah, Yahweh, Great Spirit, Lord—and his prayers were very targeted to the specific occasion at hand, composed in very plain but heartfelt language. An example occurred with the "Blessing of I-70 Road and Railroad Tracks and Builders" that was offered as construction began on elevating a major interstate highway along the border of Martin's property.[79] The acceptance of this construction was in stark contrast to the Father Hardin's righteous anger against the construction of another highway, I-65, earlier in his days at Holy Angels. On the second occasion, he called together his staff to pray with him. His prayer was composed in call and response fashion, with "Let us pray to the Lord, Lord have mercy" as the response. The various petitions asked for the safety of the construction workers and bystanders, for travelers, for truckers who need sleep, for the children in the neighborhood "that they will not test themselves by climbing the sand unto the road," for the neighborhood residents that would have to bear the sound of traffic after the road was elevated, and finally, for Martin University, that the construction not impede its work.

Martin Center College and its successor, Martin University, had always been called a "healing environment," primarily because the vision was to enable students who previously had felt excluded from higher education and discounted by society to feel successful and confident of their self-worth. Father Boniface and Sister Jane's long-term interest in physical health added a more concrete dimension to the healing environment. One legacy of their involvement in the Sickle Cell Center had been their commitment to genetics, which formed the basis for an important interest area at Martin. Another was the emphasis on health services in the college, which expanded over the years from a part-time nurse to two full-time nurses and the implementation of a robust community health services program at Martin. Through partnerships with various community organizations and health-service providers, Martin came to serve not only its own student body, but also the surrounding Martindale-Brightwood community with such services as hypertension screening, mammograms, prostate testing, tobacco cessation and substance abuse counseling, domestic violence prevention, and health education services. These services, developed with the expertise of Doctor Ray Pierce, who had also assisted with the establishment of the Sickle Cell Center, were an important component of Martin's educational program.

In addition to the health programs, Martin also had programs in community educational outreach. For example, the College Avenue campus was the site of GED and literacy programs for community members and parolees. Martin charged no rent for the organizers of these programs and helped to administer their foundation grants at no cost. In 1990 the Etheridge Knight House, named for the first poet laureate of Martin, was established as the site of many community outreach activities. Martin hosted activities such as United Parcel Service recruiting or Chamber of Commerce meetings to situate them within the community context. Although the university was nonsectarian, it scheduled annual events such as the liturgy celebrating the feast day of Saint Martin de Porres or holidays of other religions. Additionally, Martin hosted youth programs and cultural events open to all Indianapolis area residents, but most specifically, to those in Martindale-Brightwood. Over time, Father Hardin recognized that ministers in the community also needed education; he often gave religious leaders full scholarships, believing that their continuing education would have a far-reaching impact on their congregations. Father Hardin came to term Martin, the "communiversity," a university that served its entire community.[80]

One signature program offered regularly at Martin University was the Frederick Douglass reenactments. Father Hardin was accustomed to hearing others say that he bore a physical resemblance to the renowned orator and abolitionist. He told the story of being asked, upon meeting members of Douglass's family in Washington, DC, and Indianapolis, if he was related to them.[81] During a White House tour, Father Hardin came across President Bill Clinton, who acted as though he had seen a ghost. "I know who you are! You're Frederick Douglass!" Clinton exclaimed.[82] Father Hardin developed such a respect for the man that he carefully studied his life and works, amassing a collection of photos and artifacts associated with Douglass. "Frederick Douglass was an apologist for America," he observed. "We who are priests and evangelists are apologists for truth. We deal with people on this level. I see the Christ figure in Frederick Douglass. He was a minister after he got free from slavery."[83]

In 1994, working with nine students, Father Hardin began performances that made Douglass come to life for the community. Aided by Sister Jane's background research, he became an expert on the life of Douglass and created a Frederick Douglass room at Martin, complete with photographs and artifacts. Visitors to Martin as well as students and staff were treated to personal tours as Father told the story of Douglass's life. The performances, held at Martin as well as in community venues such as schools and libraries, depicted significant moments in the life of Douglass as well as some creative possibilities, such as a dialogue between Douglass and Martin Luther King Jr. Father Hardin purchased period costumes and delighted in dressing as Douglass. Planning for the performances was more of an educational event than enactment of a script. Father Hardin gathered those who were to be involved, primarily Martin staff members, and told them about the event or theme they were to portray, instructing them to research what their characters would have done or said. Sister Jane provided in-depth historical research and sources for each of the performers to pursue. The group would come together at intervals to develop a loose script, which was not written down in any detail. As Gardner, who played Douglass's wife Anna, recalled of Father Hardin's approach: "He did not want a script. He wanted you to become immersed into it just like he was into Frederick Douglass."[84]

A dress rehearsal was held to iron out trouble spots or design new additions. Performances were thus somewhat improvised, giving them a freshness and creative quality. Father Hardin liked to juxtapose actual historical events with current themes as well, imagining how the past and present would in-

Father Boniface Hardin as Frederick Douglass, circa 2000.

Father Hardin repeating Frederick Douglass's words in Pendleton, Indiana. "I attracted the fury of the mob, which laid me prostrate on the ground with a torrent of blows . . . leaving me thus, with my right hand broken, and in a state of unconsciousness."

teract. The performances included such topics as Frederick Douglass Brings Dred Scott to an Ol' Camp Meeting, Abolitionists and Suffragists Meet at an Ol' Colored Convention, Frederick Douglass Brings Dr. Martin Luther King, Jr. and Minister Malcolm X to a Treaty Signing between the North and South, Frederick Douglass Goes on Trial, Frederick Douglass Recalls the Presidents of His Lifetime, and An Anti-Slavery Meeting at Pendleton, Indiana.

Father's goal was both to pay homage to Douglass and to educate. In the program to the Pendleton performance, he wrote: "We have sought to provide a look at history that is entertaining and, at the same time, befitting an institution of higher education."[85] Both performers and audience emerged from the experience with a deeper understanding of Douglass and U.S. history. The printed programs for the events described the incidents to be portrayed, often quoting at length from Douglass's works and describing the characters who were present. Each performance included songs relevant to the topic, drawn from spirituals, patriotic songs, or even folk songs. Audience involvement was cultivated through singing, reacting to the events, and praying afterward for the spread of freedom. The popular performances were first offered in the old Saint Francis de Sales Church, which was being used for theater studies, and later in the Gathertorium. They were free and open to the public.

Other cultural events at Martin over the years included the Phillips Band Concerts, productions of *Medea* and *An Evening with Edgar Allen Poe*, a poetry reading by Nikki Giovanni, productions of *Porgy and Bess* and *Beowulf*, lectures by Sister Helen Prejean on the death penalty, boxer Rubin "Hurricane" Carter on wrongful imprisonment, and Susan Taylor, editor of *Essence* magazine, on entrepreneurship. The facility was filled regularly with members of the community eager to meet and learn from celebrities, be uplifted by music or theater, or educated by lectures on contemporary topics. Father Hardin believed that Martin should be an educational center in the broad sense, enriching the surrounding community as well as its student population.

Financial strain was a characteristic of Martin during Father Hardin's lifetime. Like all tuition-dependent private schools, Martin's financial health was tied to enrollment, grants, and donations. On several occasions, cash flow jeopardized payroll and Father Hardin was forced to go hat-in-hand to friends of Martin, notably Bill Mays, president of Mays Chemical, or Gene Sease, former president of the University of Indianapolis and chairman of Sease, Gerig, and Associates, an Indianapolis communications and consulting firm. These friends advanced short-term loans or agreed to guarantee bank loans. In addition, Father Hardin developed a close relationship with these and other benefactors, which proved to be very important for the life of the institution. He also was able to draw on the talents of Martin University friends such as Jim Morris, influential political figure, businessman, and one-time president of the Indiana Pacers basketball team, and David Kelly, president of the Indianapolis water utility, who each chaired important capital campaigns. Father Hardin was also on good terms with officeholders such as U.S. Representative Julia Carson, Indiana State Senator Glenn Howard, and Indiana House

Sister Jane Schilling (left), Reverend Tommy Brown (center), and Sister Helen Prejean (right), author of Dead Men Walking, *during Prejean's visit to Martin University in 2002.*

Representatives Bill Crawford and John Bartlett, who helped obtain important grants and donations. Some of these friendships involved smoothing over past differences from the time when Father Hardin was engaged in protest activity against the police, mayor, and governor. One touching incident occurred when Mayor Richard Lugar's former deputy and a Martin supporter, Michael Carroll, died in an airplane accident in 1992. At the funeral, the mayor and Father Hardin embraced, vowing to work together, rather than remaining at odds with each other.

Although fund-raising was an activity that Father Hardin did not like to do, his natural gregariousness and interest in people helped him to establish strong relationships with donors and foundations. During his presidency, more than $20 million in gifts and grants were obtained for Martin. By far, most foundation support came from the Lilly Endowment, which made planning grants, provided funds for several programs such as the Urban Ministries Program and youth and college preparatory summer programs, and supported the construction of a new education center at the Avondale campus. In total, Lilly grants accounted for almost $11 million over the years. Other foundations targeted specific initiatives, such as the Moriah Fund, which supported the psychology and early childhood education programs; the Lumina Foundation, which funded strategic planning; and the Noyes Memorial Foundation, which funded capital projects. During Father Hardin's tenure, Martin received only modest funding through corporate gifts and grants, with the Independent Colleges of Indiana making the most important regular gifts over the years. US Filter, NiSource, Fifth Third Bank, and TWC Resources were among those who contributed between $50,000 and $100,000.

Several individual donors made annual donations during the Father Hardin years. Most of the substantial donations were given during the capital campaign of 2001–02, but a core of more consistent donors contributed over the years. Major gifts were made by the Michael Browning family, Duane and Fern Winger (Sister Jane's sister and brother-in-law), Mays, Allen and Roberta Wurzman, Louise Fulton, Stan and Sandy Hunt, and Anne Ayres Taylor. Although efforts were made to solicit alumni and board of trustee contributions, the results were often very limited. Alumni often had modest incomes and trustees were generally appointed from Father Hardin's close circle of associates, rather than from the ranks of the wealthy.

Father Hardin's colleagues with experience in philanthropy attributed the lack of more corporate and individual support to Father Hardin's reluctance to spend more of his time in fund-raising and his modesty in asking for only small amounts of money. Charles Blair, former officer with the Lilly Foundation, said, "He felt sometimes like he was a beggar. He'd say that: 'I hate to beg.' And I'd say, 'Father, you're not begging. This is an institution.'"[86] Mays, a key benefactor, told of a humorous incident that illustrates Father Hardin's unease with fund-raising. On a visit to ask Mays for help to maintain some of the College Avenue buildings, Father offered him a flu shot from the Martin clinic, claiming that he wanted to give him something in return. Mays quickly turned down the opportunity for reciprocation.[87] One possible explanation for Father's reluctance with respect to fund-raising was his personal lifestyle. As a priest and monk, he lived according to a vow of poverty. He took only a small salary, paid through the monastery and enough to support only his very modest daily expenses, donating the remainder back to Martin. In the annual listing of the *Chronicle of Higher Education,* which regularly reports the salaries of university presidents, Father Hardin achieved the distinction of being the lowest paid in the country (officially, zero dollars for salary per year).[88] His lack of financial resources never prevented him from action; he was confident that funds would materialize when needed. This faith was a part of his spirituality, an expression of trust in God and detachment from material things. To fundraisers intent on building endowments and accruing funds before enacting new programs, Father's approach was frustrating. Blair, for example, urged Father Hardin to accrue interest on a Lilly grant to build the Education Center by delaying construction a year so that the funds would expand. Father was eager to build, however, and used the funds quickly.[89] A second explanation for Father Hardin's failure to engage in more vigorous fund-raising was his management style, which kept him on campus and involved in everyday decisions. Rather than delegate these tasks so that he could be freed up to do more fund-raising, he chose to keep a close hand on management.

Father Hardin, Sister Jane, and the Martin faculty and staff continually wrote grants for government-sponsored programs. Most of these were relatively small grants that supported such programs as tutoring and mentoring of at-risk students (AmeriCorps), urban community service (U.S. Department of Housing and Urban Development), a summer program for urban high school students called Next Step Education through Archeology, and the Festival of Arts (Indiana Arts Commission). One successful program was called Operation FEED (Federation of Educational and Economic Development), which was funded by the Lilly Endowment. When the endowment asked Father about pressing needs, he and his staff developed a $750,000 proposal to support students directly by helping them find employment through assisting them to compose résumés, prepare for interviews, obtain internships, and locate job opportunities. The Resource Division of the program helped students pay for bus passes or other transportation needs, feed themselves and their families, or find social-service agencies to assist them and their families with specific issues. This program ran for three years and was very successful in helping students to complete their degrees and enter chosen careers. Father Hardin's choice of a program to supply basic necessities for students was indicative of his understanding of what it took for Martin students to persist. While grants allowed Martin to offer targeted programs, however, they did not support the everyday life of the institution. Consultant Gary Quehl recommended in his 2004 report that Martin cultivate more unrestricted donations to support the basic operations of the university rather than continue to focus on writing grant proposals and administering the programs that had been funded.[90]

Greenan described Father Hardin's style as that of a "benevolent dictator." He regarded the university as "his baby" and therefore regarded decision making as his personal province. Greenan also observed that both Father Hardin and Sister Jane "didn't understand the need to have advice. Neither one liked to take advice from people. Father believed, and I think Sister did too, that they were on a crusade, that they worked hard, they built a school, they started it and here were these people trying to tell them how to run it. And I think they would listen to some extent because they had to for financial aid or for some other governmental issue, but they really didn't like to take advice very well."[91]

Associates came to understand that they could present ideas to Father Hardin and argue for them, but if he had his mind set on something their words had no influence. Sister Jane had some limited impact on certain issues, but often he overruled her with an "Oh, Janey." As the person who consistently articulated the vision, Father Hardin felt strongly about the way in which it was implemented. In similar fashion, he had run-ins with staff who insisted on following protocol when Father Hardin felt that a higher priority was important. Often a hiring decision that he made on the basis of compassion or a gut feeling rather than on credentials caused a rift with Martin's personnel staff. "There are countless stories of people that he helped," Blair recalled, with "people on the staff who probably would have had a hard time finding work somewhere else. He knew them, he gave them a chance. And he did that with at least 10 or 11 people that I'm aware of, who had washed out, who had had trouble in a prior position who for some reason or another had gained the ire of their former employees. And if he believed they were sincere, he would give them a job—a job that actually did something. It wasn't like they were just here. But they would have a job and were required to perform. And normally they paid off."[92] Similarly, he regularly felt that the constraints of a funded project were preventing Martin from putting funding where it should be directed as new needs arose, so funding officials came to expect that he would routinely ask for exceptions and revisions.

Father Hardin distrusted external consultants and felt that their explorations were nothing short of prying. For example, he restricted the work of a consultant hired with funds from Lumina, Quehl, by insisting on sitting in on most interviews conducted for the project and refusing to provide certain types of information.[93] When consultants from the Noel Levitz organization were retained to make suggestions on recruitment and retention, Father Hardin dismissed their findings. He did not believe that outsiders could understand the special nature of Martin, and his single-minded drive to protect and preserve Martin occasionally was perceived as possessive and defensive.[94]

In his role as president, Father Hardin blended this control of decision making with a loving attitude. He eschewed formality in favor of a paternal approach, routinely walking the halls and engaging in discussions and joking with students, staff, and faculty. Greenan described the student-centered style of Father Hardin: "The students loved it. 'Oh, Father,' they would walk up to him in the hallway. It reminded me of the early days in Catholic school when the nuns would walk around the playground and they always had a bevy of people following them around. That was kind of like Father. He would always attract students who would talk to him a lot of times about stuff not related at all to education."[95] He welcomed visits to his office and regaled visitors with stories and lectures about various intellectual topics, such as astronomy, current events, or history. Father Hardin further established the family atmosphere through convening administrative staff meetings that were at once occasions for him to share insights on ideas he had or things he had been reading as well as hearing about the performance and news of various campus units. Most of these meetings ended with the singing of a favorite song.[96]

On several occasions, the Higher Learning Commission, noting the absence of faculty involvement in decision making or the limited authority of staff to make major changes, recommended that Father take a more participative approach. Greenan observed that when this advice was ignored repeatedly, the commission developed a tolerance, realizing that the special family ambiance of Martin rendered this central decision making more appropriate for Martin than it would be for other institutions.[97]

Several explanations can account for Father's administrative style. The father role he played mirrors descriptions of his own upbringing, with a strong father who was clearly the head of the family and in control of decisions, yet was loving and concerned with the welfare of family members. Since Martin students and faculty often described the university as a "family," the father figure was clearly Father Hardin. In addition, he was ordained at a time when priests not only were revered and given great amounts of authority and deference, but they also were expected to minister to the needs of others. Blair observed, "As you know the Catholic Church is patriarchal and so every-thing flows through the men. There's the pope, down to the priest to the local church. And so in a sense he was a patriarch."[98] Father Hardin's flexibility and responsiveness to new situations and insights led him to place less value on conformity to standard practice and protocol.

CHARLES SCHISLA

Marilyn Quayle, Father Hardin, and Archbishop Daniel Buechlein as Father Hardin receives the Spirit of Indy Award in 1995.

Although Father Hardin was very active as president in terms of vision and major decisions, he was not interested in the daily work of implementing the smaller details. His partnership with Sister Jane provided the perfect fit in this respect: Because she shared his vision and respected his authority, she was committed to carrying out the day-to-day administration involved in making sure grades were submitted and recorded, catalogues were published, and the myriad other tasks that are part of running a college were accomplished. Former trustee Tom McKenna summed up Sister Jane's role as Martin developed as a university: "She sustained all that while he was making the adjustments from dashikis to diplomas. She was going to make sure that the diploma had some credence, validity, cachet, that it wasn't hokey education, it wasn't education that didn't have substance in it."[99] Blair described the complementary nature of the relationship between the two administrators: "She helped him develop a structure that he needed to run an institution, a structure, the who's on first. And it worked because I don't think he liked that kind of stuff and I don't think he would have been very good at it, if he had to just sit up and worry about student loans like the provost has to do. He was the guiding force

Father Hardin receiving the Sagamore of the Wabash award from Lieutenant Governor Becky Skillman.

but he didn't want to deal with the minutia and she did."[100] Alumnus Bernard McFarland agreed, seeing Father Hardin as "A free spirit, free thinker. . . . If he thinks of something, he moves on it, where Sister Jane was more calculated. They were just kind of ying and yang. It was a unique relationship and I truly believe that she was a great, great support to him and a lot of his vision, she probably was able to bring a lot of his vision and allow it to be presented in a way that made sense, because sometimes people didn't understand Father Hardin, because he was a visionary and a lot of the minutia, or the detail things, probably didn't bog him down in that, where probably Sister Jane was more meticulous a person."[101]

Father Hardin's relationship with the Martin University Board of Trustees during most of his tenure was consistent with his administrative style. The first boards were composed of close associates who admired him and were eager to support his ideas. In an unusual arrangement, Father Hardin was himself considered a trustee with an official vote, rather than reporting to the board as most university presidents do. Notable leaders on the board during this period were Bobbie Beckwith, William Malone, and Jim Shaw. In time, more trustees with roots in the business community were recruited to deal with the university's always precarious financial status.

As the composition of the board changed, Father Hardin found himself disagreeing with members more frequently. Accustomed to being the strong decision maker, Father Hardin was troubled by arguments that seemed to take the university in different directions than he previously had chosen; he became impatient with board members who put money and power considerations into a new vision for Martin. As more trustees with corporate or political backgrounds were added to the board, the differences escalated. McKenna, Bill West, and Bartlett, while close friends of Father Hardin, remained concerned and focused on fiscal issues and the modernization of Martin University, while Father Hardin pursued ideas more in keeping with traditional liberal arts and community service. Most of the dissent was about money; board members were still very content to leave the academic decisions to Father Hardin and Sister Jane, but continually pressed for more attention to fund-raising. Former board chair West recalled, "He himself had reconstituted the Board. He had gone out and recruited like 10 new people to the board. And many of them were younger, and many of them were pragmatic, extremely pragmatic. And it was no longer what the Board used to be, which was five or six of his friends sitting around the table, now it was a bunch of young people wanting to know,

'Okay, what's the plan here?' And he didn't appreciate that either. Board meetings became very testy and a lot of friction and very emotional."[102]

Father Hardin had had a number of health crises, all of which he survived and turned into advocacy situations, becoming a public spokesperson for diabetes, prostate cancer, and other issues. However, as he moved into his seventies, the board began to think about succession issues, much to Father Hardin's chagrin. West indicated that the board had been urged on by other parties as well, "A lot of the funders around town started pressing Father about a succession plan. He did not like that at all. He felt that people were trying to put him in the grave."[103] The fear that his health and verve would deteriorate upon retirement was clearly a part of Father Hardin's reluctance to step down. A community survey was done, resulting in a call for succession planning, a suggestion that Father Hardin took to mean lack of confidence in his leadership. He was still feeling vital and felt that he had a lot to contribute. Sease, a friend and benefactor, recalled talking with a troubled Father Hardin about the suggestions he had been hearing from the trustees, community leaders, and staff, "He said to me, 'Gene, do you think I'm getting too old for this job?' And I said, 'No, I haven't noticed it.' And he said, . . . 'when you get to my age, you have folks saying to you, 'How are you feeling?' or 'Are you thinking about retirement?' And he said "That's what they're doing to me. . . . People are thinking there's a need for new leadership there.' And he was despondent."[104]

Father Hardin participated in several walks for health issues, such as this one for sickle-cell anemia.

MARTIN CENTER SICKLE CELL INITIATIVE

Sease suggested, among other things, that Father Hardin shave off his beard to look younger. The beard was long a bone of contention between Father Hardin and his mother, Elizabeth, who often told her son she wanted to see his face. In reply, he jokingly told her that he had a few more people to scare before he shaved it off. However, the combination of his mother's wish and Sease's suggestion led to what was a momentous occasion to many in Father Hardin's life—the shaving of the beard in 2003. When he arrived at Martin for his first day without a beard, the shock waves traveled not only throughout the university but also the city. Father Hardin made up several humorous stories to explain his decision to be clean-shaven, that he could now play a younger Frederick Douglass.

Despite the new appearance, inquiries into Father's retirement plans continued. Former trustee Gary Gibson remembered differences of opinion on the board: "There were people who didn't want him to go, and there were people who thought, well, maybe he should go because he's tired, and we don't want to wear him out, and then there were some people who said well, we need to do a new direction and that was a small percentage."[105] West observed that pressure to develop a succession plan emanated as well from the foundations that contributed to Martin. Some faculty and staff were also feeling that new leadership would create a fresh vision for Martin, more modern with respect to use of technology, larger and more prominent as an institution. Reluctantly, Father Hardin agreed to engage in strategic planning and the formulation of a succession plan, activities that were funded by the Lumina Foundation.

The process began with workshop sessions for the planning team in fall 2004, facilitated by consultants hired with the Lumina funds. Among these were Quehl, Jim Minor, Ron Wendeln, Bill Bergquist, and John Phillips. The primary consultant, Quehl, began by using an appreciative inquiry strategy, which focused on the strengths of the institution. Through interviews and town hall meetings, he elicited themes that were articulated in his report to the university and in a book of Martin University accomplishments issued by the university. As this summary of strengths and accomplishments was completed, the work of planning for the future began. Committees worked on different topics such as environmental scanning; their reports and the recommendations of the consultants were blended into a draft of the strategic plan. The planning process involved some forty-eight people. Additional meetings with the various Martin constituents took place over the course of the next year and the plan was approved by the board of trustees in October 2005.

MARTIN UNIVERSITY

Father Hardin in his office shortly after shaving off his famous beard.

Throughout the process, Father Hardin had conflicting feelings: he was intent on documenting and preserving a tradition that would outlast him, yet reluctant to yield his leadership. He personally conducted many of the meetings that led to the strategic plan and closely monitored the consultants.

The strategic plan itself reflected the foundational beliefs of Martin University: the focus on low-income, minority, or nontraditional students; the sustaining of a healing and freedom-minded environment; and the goal of giving each graduate the power to think and plan for lives of service and success. Most of the specific goals, with the exception of the pursuit of establishing the first doctoral program in counseling psychology, were continuations and extensions of existing ideas and practices. The succession plan called for the board of trustees to set up a process for conducting the search for a new president, to begin in January 2008.[106]

Father Hardin and Sister Jane set the date of their retirement as December 31, 2007. During the planning process, it became clear that both had health issues. Father had recovered from prostate cancer surgery in 2003 but was having some incidents where he would suddenly lose track of what he was saying and fall asleep, possibly due to mini strokes. Sister Jane had been hospitalized with heart and organ infections and was experiencing the early signs of Alzheimer's. Father Hardin protected her fiercely and tried his best to avoid

FATHER BONIFACE HARDIN COLLECTION, INDIANA HISTORICAL SOCIETY

Indianapolis mayor Bart Peterson presents Father Hardin with an honorary street sign.

putting her into situations where her memory lapses would be noticed. As he coped with her illness and the heartache that accomplished this development, retirement most likely became more warranted. His most trusted colleague, the person who embraced his vision and turned it into reality in so many ways, was becoming increasingly incapacitated. The team that built Martin was being heavily tested by age and disability. An anguished Father Hardin prayed for guidance and acceptance. As the time neared for retirement, Father and Sister became more gracious about leaving and tried to define positive ways in which they could continue to support Martin and do other good work. In a 2004 interview Father Hardin said, "When my time comes and I have to step aside as President . . . there will be life in me. I think my life after this life is going to be about healing. There are so many wounded people in this world."[107]

A retirement celebration featured tributes from key government leaders, higher education officials, and civil rights leaders. Sister Jane recounted the history of Martin with anecdotes and humor, while Father Hardin exhorted participants to love themselves and serve others. He outlined some plans for the future, saying he was "stepping aside," not retiring. His plans included continuing advocacy work for prostate and breast cancer and Alzheimer's, teaching metaphysics, and his newest advocacy focus: children. He talked about "our babies" suffering from abuse, dying of neglect and poverty, passionately urging those at the celebration "to claim these babies as our own."[108] Characteristically, he ended the ceremony with the singing of "Oh, Freedom."

As the succession plan had stipulated, the board of trustees and university cabinet contracted with a search firm to identify candidates for the presidency of Martin University. The search involved members of the Martin faculty, staff, and community in writing a position description and recruiting and screening candidates. Father Hardin took part in the process and did not hesitate to voice his opinions: when the first narrowing of the list of candidates to five finalists did not include his favorite candidate, he protested until that person was added back to the list. As the board of trustees announced its final choice, Father Hardin was chagrined to hear that Algeania Freeman, a candidate he did not favor, was chosen, but vowed to work with her.

With Father Hardin and Sister Jane's departure, an incredible era of growth and productivity at Martin ended. Amidst a chorus of naysayers, they had managed to found an accredited institution of higher education. They had created fine academic programs, health and cultural resources for the Martindale-Brightwood and the entire Indianapolis community, graduated 1,370 students, and been a moral force in Indiana. Although they had regrets about retiring, the mood of Sister Jane and Father Hardin was celebratory; they were proud of their accomplishments and looking forward to new initiatives. Unknown to anyone, what was to come was the most painful period in Father Hardin and Sister Jane's lives.

Chapter 5

"Only the love, that's all we can take with us after we leave. We can't take the hate because God won't let you in. Only the love."[1]

As 2008 began Father Boniface Hardin and Sister Jane Shilling retired to their respective homes and began to plan their postretirement activities. They lived with their beloved dogs—Father Hardin's Eternity and Sister Jane's Frieda—in simple ranch homes in the same subdivision, homes they had originally bought and later deeded over to Martin University. Having, for the past thirty years, donated the bulk of their salaries into an endowment account that totaled more than $600,000 (most of which had been borrowed back by the university), they reached a retirement agreement that would pay each of them $30,000 per year as a retirement pension, with half of this amount set aside for maintenance of their homes and automobiles, health insurance, and other routine expenses. The remaining $15,000 was paid to their respective religious organizations, since they had taken vows of poverty. The religious organizations then dispensed what funds they needed for daily living. They were to be allowed to continue to live in their homes and use Martin cars.[2]

The next task was to determine what Father Hardin and Sister Jane would do in retirement. In an interview just before he left his post, Father Hardin spoke about his concern for helping children who are hurt and those with cancer. "It is my theological opinion that until we start treating these babies and children the way they should be treated there will be no peace on this Earth," he said.[3] Father Hardin also talked about assisting the new president and continuing to teach occasionally.

As winter passed, Father Hardin and Sister Jane busied themselves making lists of the many ways in which they would continue to serve and to grow. A central organizing principle espoused by Father was "Hagia Sophia," or Holy Wisdom, a "norm and goal for the rest of our lives. Anything that does not come under this title receives a 'no'—internally and externally for it offends God."[4] He intended to continue to study language each day, listing the thirteen languages he knew in addition to English and noting the degree of competence and kind of knowledge he had in each, whether biblical, liturgical, spoken, or written.[5] He and Sister had an active prayer life; they structured their days

around prayer and listed a morning, noon, evening, and daily scripture schedule. One day each month was to be set aside as "Heaven's Day," a day of special
readings and prayers for their eventual passing.

Father Hardin and Sister Jane's plans also included health-care topics, such
as the resolves to take their medications, see physicians at the proper time,
and have dental and medical checkups. They anticipated involvement in religious services, such as masses at the Carmelite Monastery or parishes that requested Father Hardin's presence, and wakes and funeral services. In addition
to Father Hardin's planned biography, "Pickin' Cotton on the Way to Church,"
and the history of Martin University, they intended to write several books,
essays, and speeches with titles such as the "Future of Higher Learning,"
"Andragogy as the Language of Higher Education," "Preparation for Learning
in Early Childhood," "The Twelve Apostles," and "Future Civilization: Change
or Annihilation." Father Hardin planned to continue his Frederick Douglass
reenactments and to do additional research on Douglass's life. He and Sister
Jane wanted to evaluate the requests that they had received to serve on the
boards of community organizations. In addition to the work of establishing
a campaign against abused children, they vowed to "be prepared for new and
innovative ideas—even those that are different or opposed to our own."[6] But
their plans for a peaceful life of writing, continued service, and prayer were
rudely interrupted.

To their dismay, Father Hardin and Sister Jane soon began receiving reports of significant changes at Martin. Father Hardin's hope that he would be
able to assist with a smooth transition to new leadership was dashed when the
new president, Algeania Freeman, barred him and Sister Jane from campus.
Freeman began to make rapid changes at Martin, reducing faculty and staff,
eliminating programs, changing the enrollment demographics, and removing
photos of the founders. In time, the majority of the members of the Board of
Trustees resigned. Martin had fewer connections with the community.[7] As
they learned of these events, Father Hardin and Sister Jane became extremely
agitated and anguished over how to address the changes.[8]

Isolated from the university they loved, Father Hardin and Sister Jane received visitors who brought information about the changes on campus. They
consoled those who had lost their positions and offered advice on the multiple lawsuits that were being prepared by those fired. They both experienced
profound sorrow on learning that several former staff members had become
disloyal and spoke unfavorably about the former mission and practices of

Martin. The events had a crushing effect on all. They perceived that the institution that they had dreamed of, the one that they had built year by year and dollar by dollar, was now out of their hands and changing drastically.

Father Hardin and Sister Jane had no recourse but to watch helplessly. They made a habit of regularly driving around the perimeter of the school, viewing the buildings and wondering how their dream had slipped away. "I think that was something he had to do for his own good. I think it broke his heart to not be able to go into the building," Billie Glenn said. "That he had begged, borrowed and got everybody to give money to build it. . . . And for him not to be able to get into it, it just was something that slowly tapped him down."[9] Former Lilly Endowment and Martin staff member Charles Blair described the state of affairs: "Oh, he was sad. He was just sad. I think he kind of didn't understand it because he's not that way [unkind]. So it's very surprising to people who are kind and you would think well, they're old and they ought to know better, but it's like when people are unkind to them, they never get used to it. They never figure that out, like why would you do that? And I think that was his question all along, was why? And I don't think anybody ever told him, to my knowledge, gave him a good reason, why he was barred from the institution and he couldn't come over here. . . . That broke his heart. I think he had faith that it [Martin] was going to survive that, but he didn't see that, he didn't know that. He was worried."[10]

Documents that Father wrote during this period reveal his state of mind. He struggled mightily to understand the situation and the personality of the new president, her motives, and her character. He vowed for his own mental health to "limit myself to three discussions daily about Dr. Freeman," to "always end [phone calls] with supporting language and encouragement," and to pray daily for Freeman.[11] Sister Jane recalled that Father Hardin urged acceptance when others called for retaliation of any sort: "He said 'You can't do that. You have to let it go.' And there were some things that we didn't like at all and he just said 'That's something you have to bear. You cannot tear it apart. Remember we put it together, but you can't be part of tearing it apart.'"[12] John Gibson observed, "He didn't express rancor and vindictiveness. He said to me several times, 'I'm trying to be forgiving, I'm trying to understand what she's [Freeman] up to and hoping it will be for the best.'"[13] At the same time, Father Hardin was wary that there would be violence, that there would be several legal suits, and even that Freeman would go so far as to try to have him arrested.[14]

To some, the administrative changes were warranted. Over the years, Father Hardin's compassion and belief in the ability of others to learn and thrive had led him to hire several staff members who did not have the credentials or experience for their positions. He saw in these people the desire to perform and a loyalty and commitment to Martin, qualities that superseded their limited backgrounds. Freeman was intent on improving the financial status of Martin and taking the university in a more traditional direction. She wanted to increase enrollment and bring in more funding, so she turned to programs that would fill the school even though they would change its character. The turmoil that accompanied the changes was extensive.

In retrospect, some supporters of the university regretted the decisions that had taken place. Some felt that Father Hardin should not have been urged to retire. Blair exemplified this position: "I don't think it was handled very well. I think there was some sense that he was getting older and he never would retire unless the board pushed him, and that probably was true. I don't think he was ready to go at the time he retired. And quite frankly, I don't think he should have retired at the time he retired. I think the Board was wrong."[15]

After nearly three years, Freeman retired in December 2010.[16] In December of 2010 Charlotte Westerhaus-Renfrow, previously vice president of diversity and inclusion at the National Collegiate Athletic Association, assumed the role of interim president. While at the NCAA, then-President Myles Brand had taken her to Martin to meet Father Hardin, a man he revered, saying, "You will not be effective in your role here at the NCAA until you meet Father Boniface Hardin."[17] She was extremely impressed by the visit and felt that she could restore the role of Father Hardin when the board asked her to step in.

Westerhaus-Renfrow immediately set about trying to mend the relationships that had been broken during the previous administration.[18] She welcomed Father Hardin and Sister Jane back to the campus, setting up office space for them. At first, Father Hardin was angry and suspicious of the new president. He was heartbroken when he walked through his old office and the Frederick Douglass room and found that it had been gutted. In time, however, he came to trust the interim president. She welcomed him to speak at homecoming and graduation and worked to restore the honor accorded to the founding president and Sister Jane. Westerhaus-Renfrow held a large meeting of community leaders, church leaders, social workers, and others in the Martindale-Brightwood community to welcome them back to campus.

At the end of August 2011, Westerhaus-Renfrow remembered saying good-bye to Father and Sister as they left the building. He was wearing a bright blue suit, the suit he wore when he was especially happy. "I was at one end of the hallway and they had already said our goodbyes and for some reason, I turned around and I watched him and Sister Jane slowly walk down that hallway," Westerhaus-Renfrow remembered. "And they just leaned into one another and were nodding and talking and for some reason, he must have felt me and he turned around and smiled. And then they walked out the door."[19] An assistant told Westerhaus-Renfrow that Father Hardin said he was tired and probably would not be in during the next week. That would be his last visit to Martin.

Three years after the firings at Martin, Father Hardin and Sister Jane were still counseling twenty or so people to see if they could be reinstated or find other placements. Exhausted from the efforts and emotionally drained, Father later recalled that he had the sense that one night in September 2011 President Barack Obama was going to be assassinated. He had anguished over this before bedtime. Around 4:00 a.m. he woke up to use the bathroom and collapsed in the hallway, felled by a stroke. He tried to crawl to a telephone but was unable and lay there until the following morning when Sister Jane and a nearby friend and student, Alice Gwynn, entered the home when he failed to show up for church. They found him unresponsive and called emergency workers, who transported him to the hospital. His left side had been affected, yet after receiving initial care in the hospital he recovered consciousness.[20]

Father Hardin was moved to a convalescent center and received continuing physical therapy. He had a few setbacks that required repeated hospitalization and relocation to other centers. The focus was on strengthening his left side and building his stamina. Sister Jane, assisted by former staff member and now loyal caregiver, Stefanie Lee, visited every day. At first Father Hardin was resolute about making a full recovery. He began work to explore stoke as a medical condition, intending to campaign in the black community about stroke prevention in the same way as he had advocated for prostate cancer awareness. He also renewed his intention to create a movement to counter child abuse. Father Hardin asked visitors to bring him information that he could use to pursue these causes. Several friends came to see Father Hardin regularly, yet life at the rehabilitation centers was isolating and controlled.

To his dismay, Father's condition continued to deteriorate. Yet, he did not feel that his mission was over and struggled to remain active. In a wheelchair, he made two appearances at Martin, one on his birthday on November 18 and the other for a fund-raising event. For every upturn, however, there seemed to be a setback. As he experienced more damaging episodes, he came to recognize that the end might be near. He had some visions in which departed people called to him and promised to guide him home. He secured a promise from the author that she would do her best to write his biography and met with legal advisers and family members about important life affairs.

Gradually, Father Hardin was able to respond only faintly. Westerhaus-Renfrow recalled visiting him after it had been announced that another candidate, rather than she, had been chosen as the next president of Martin: "I told him, 'I'm really sorry. I really worked hard. I really wanted you to be proud of me.' And then this tear came down his face but he wasn't really moving. I didn't know if the tear was the aftereffects of stroke. So on my way out the door, I asked the nurse, 'Can he hear me?' and she said, 'He can hear you.' And I told her what happened and she said, 'Oh, he reacts, he just can't talk.' So she said, 'Probably that tear was him hearing you.'"[21]

The new president of Martin, George Miller, came to visit Father Hardin in early 2012. Father received him cordially and they had a short conversation. Sister Jane and Lee continued to minister to Father and a smaller flow of visitors came regularly. It was clear that Father was on his final journey. In March he contracted pneumonia and was semiconscious, breathing with difficulty but in peace. On March 24, when the doctor informed Sister Jane that Father Boniface was nearing death, she lowered the bed so that Sister could hold him and left her in the room with him. As Sister Jane held Father Hardin, she saw a small monk come into the room and anoint Father Hardin, who had already been anointed earlier. The doctor and Lee, who were waiting across the hall and preventing others from interrupting, saw no one enter. They regarded this as a final vision and indication of Father's passing.[22]

Father Hardin chose to be buried in his monk's clothing. He was celebrated at Martin and at a funeral Mass that filled the Cathedral of Saints Peter and Paul of the Archdiocese of Indianapolis on March 29, 2012. His body was later brought to Saint Meinrad Archabbey to be interred with the other deceased Benedictine monks in a grave marked by a simple cross. Tributes came from every corner. Trustee and Director of the Sickle Cell Center Gary Gibson summed up the thinking of many: "I for one believe that everyone is given gifts, and everyone starts with gifts, others may acquire them as they go, but some people actually get a whole package of gifts, and he was one of those;

and great for him, great for us that knew him and those of us who benefited from his presence. . . . There are certain things that it was determined that he was going to have to accomplish, and he was outfitted for that." [23]

Assessing a Life: Father Hardin through His Words and the Words of Those Who Knew Him

Although he was an excellent writer, Father Hardin was, most of all, a "people person." He was outgoing and always on the move; his administrative office, his home, even his campus, were too small to contain his energy. He thrived on interactions with students, community leaders, colleagues, and other community members. His talks were from the heart and often quite impromptu. Although some of his words were captured through video and audio, he did not commit much to writing. He spoke of a book of poems that he wrote, called "Monkish Melodies," but no copies have yet been found. He intended to write several books and essays during his retirement, but these projects were never executed. Much of his story, then, is embedded in the memories of those with whom he came into contact. They, along with some of the preserved words of Father Hardin, are the sources for the descriptions of his character in this final section of his biography.

PHOTO BY JOHN SHERMAN

Memorial service for Father Hardin, March 28, 2012.

Father Hardin was tall, several inches over six feet. Perhaps his most striking characteristic, when added to his height, was his hair. In early photos it is dark and close-cropped. During his activist years, it blossomed into a small Afro, and then a larger one. In time a beard was added and the Afro grew more and more wild. With age, the hair and beard turned white; he appeared to be peering out of a fluffy white cloud. When he shaved his beard, the wild cloud of white hair remained, puffing out from his academic cap, topping all the heads in a given gathering, signaling his presence as he entered a room.

When Father Hardin first came to Indianapolis, his good looks were the talk of the parishes where he worked and visited. Young girls were struck by his appearance and quickly turned him into an idol. Those close to him recalled with humor that they established a protectionist stance to keep women away from Father Hardin.[24] Secretaries and other assistants ensured that they accompanied female visitors into his office and monitored their comings and goings.

The many who remarked that Father Hardin resembled his beloved hero, Frederick Douglass, were doubtlessly commenting on his height and hair, but the shape of his face and the glint of his eye were also similar. Father Hardin had an easy smile, a humble, almost folksy, speaking style, and an unexpectedly soft voice. He was quick to laughter and very focused on the person to whom he was speaking. John Day recalled, "When he talked with people, he really gave you his attention. It wasn't like shake hands, and turn your head and speak to two more people and forget you."[25] In a guest appearance at a local university to talk about "creating a welcoming culture in higher education classrooms," Father Hardin used his first hour to move from one student to another, holding them in his gaze and asking them what they hoped to accomplish in life.[26] The students quickly received a memorable message about the personal approach used at Martin University. Father Hardin was more of the kindly grandfather in interpersonal situations, although he could assume a stern and commanding presence, which he displayed often in his younger days.

Father Hardin initially wore standard clerical clothing when he first came to Indianapolis, sporting a Roman collar and a black suit. As he worked through the Black Pride and activist years, he turned to dashikis and wore colorful African robes to celebrate Mass. His love of these colorful robes continued throughout his life, even when business suits became his most frequent attire as President of Martin University. He loved color and often wore bright suits, shirts, and ties. When Father Hardin was laid to rest in his monk's hooded robe and rope cincture, it was the first time that most of those who knew him had seen him in these subdued vestments. For many, he was larger than life—literally and figuratively.

In his own mind, Father Hardin was first and foremost, Boniface the priest and monk.

- I'm Boniface, priest, monk, healer, I'm a healer, I don't smack people down, I pray over them. I do it often, several times. My prayer life is very important to me and if it were not for God, none of this could be done.[27]
- [Our call to ministry] allows us to be touched by God and find ourselves doing things we never thought we would do. I never stop being a priest in whatever I do. . . . What's my real contribution? It's my priesthood. I hope wherever I go when I've said something to people, I thought about being a priest. It's a good compliment when people say he's a good man—but a good priest [is something even more special]. We're missing the boat if we just tell stories. We must give witness.[28]
- Gene Sease recalled that "Boniface never lost his ordination as a monk. He was an educator, but he was primarily a priest. I think if you had to prioritize: was he an administrator, was he an educator, was he a priest? I think the priest would come out on top. Because he never forgot his role as a servant. He was a servant of the people."[29]

To those around him, Father Hardin embodied many of the characteristics they associated with loving and holy priests, and his ministry was united with his role as college administrator:

- If a person would come to Boniface and say, "Well, I'm not sure I'm going to be able to continue here [as a Martin student]. We're running short on money, my washer has quit working and I have four children and no husband," Boniface would say, "Well, I'll buy you a washer." And he did. He ran a little mini Med Check place for a long time there [a type of urgent care clinic at Martin] because people were hurting. They had physical problems, they needed their feet massaged, or needed some health issue, so he hired nurses and had them on duty to do that. So when I say he never lost the dedication he had as a monk, [I mean] he was more than an administrator.[30]
- I had tremendous tragedy in my life a couple of times and he was—the way he dealt with me was not like a counselor, he was like a friend. And he kind of understood that being a friend of somebody was really probably

all they needed. They didn't need a lot of advice or any of that. And I think he was probably like that with more than me, with other people, and he just he could see if there was pain, how he might serve you and that I valued a lot because there were times when he just knew that I was having trouble, whatever, and others, and he would just know that. He would be a priest; in that sense, he was a priest. He would say, "Okay, why don't you just take your time and get better? And if there is anything I can do, I'll do it." And that's the way he was.[31]

- It wasn't an unusual thing for him to get out and go if someone needed him. When he would go and comfort the sick, when he would go and anoint them so that the family would be at peace.[32]

- People really saw him, as he was, a kind of kindly priest, and that's what he was, he was a kindly, gentle priest, a gentle soul.[33]

Although Father Hardin felt a deep sorrow that the Catholic Church had participated in slavery, had embodied institutional racism, had failed to act in fighting discrimination, and had actually tried to restrain him in his work for social justice, he loved his Church. From his early days as an altar boy filled with awe as he participated in the Mass to his days of celebrating Mass throughout the parishes of Indianapolis and elsewhere, he loved the message, the moral teachings, and the traditions of the Catholic Church. During his time as a diocesan priest, he became most sensitive to the racism within the Church, and he was not sure that it would change:

- The study of the Catholic Church history in America and Indiana revealed to me that any major change of attitude toward Black people in America would not be derived from its Catholic priests, sisters and brothers. For the most part, the Catholic clergy identified with the racism of America. The master/slave relationship was constantly upheld.[34]

- I like my church, you know, it's what I grew up in. And . . . they're nice people and the only problem is I . . . I just wish they could see, you know, and just take the Gospel and the teachings, you know, it says here we're supposed to love and we're supposed to take care of our neighbor and sometimes get slapped on one cheek and have to turn another one. And I'm telling you, that's not easy. But, you know, you have to be a person of faith.[35]

- The minister who wishes to proclaim Christ's truth has to acknowledge that he is not perfect, nor are his fellow servants, but that his primary job is to teach others to love. It would be untrue if I said that the Church has the answer or that it is the "end all and be all" for Black people; it's surely not so, if actions are the measure.[36]

- The human component of the Church must be willing to be healed, taught, and—most of all—willing to learn not to be a part of oppression.[37]

As he grew older, Father Hardin's anger toward the Catholic Church cooled. Reflecting on his exodus from Holy Angels Parish, he said, "I began to realize that anger is a self-aggrandizing experience. We had to find other ways to deal with our indignity because anger just led to more anger."[38] His newfound calmness led to forgiveness: "The spirit of a true follower and imitator of Christ is to forgive and hope, and this I think I have. I forgive my Church for the deeds perpetrated against my people by its bishops, priests and sisters, and hope that someday it will be converted to Christ and His love. The shame of it is that I, too, participated in all of this somehow, just by being a part of the system."[39]

Over the years, Father Hardin leaned more on the contemplative methods of his Benedictine foundation and realized that through prayer, reflection on Scripture, and meditation, he could take action to promote change from within the Church. He urged others to become reformers, saying, "The Church, if it becomes relevant, can be a vehicle to effect changes (in the relationship between the races). But will the Church wait until there is a revolution or will it act now? . . . The Church has paid lip service to racism. We have to take the lead. We, the people, have to make the changes. It doesn't help to leave the Church. We have to stay and work."[40]

As he aged, Father found himself being more careful in his actions, while being more radical in his thinking. He said, "Sometimes when you're in the position like I am you want to do things. When I was younger I just did them and then I withstood the acrimony and harsh words against me, but when you get a little older you find yourself being a little bit more conservative. I think I'm more revolutionary in my thoughts, but I just don't want to fight the Church. It will be distracting if I say something publicly, and I have done that but it will not be helpful for me nor the Church."[41]

Although he was a Catholic priest, Father Hardin celebrated all religions in the spirit of the ecumenism of Vatican II. His activism at Holy Angels and throughout the Indianapolis community brought him into contact with leaders of many faiths, most of whom were ministers in black Protestant churches.

He deliberately downplayed his Catholic affiliation in contexts where he felt it would be a barrier, wearing African garb instead of the Roman collar, invoking the names of the deity in the terms used by various traditions. As Imam Mikal Saahir recalled, he first was attracted to Father Hardin in hearing the opening prayer on Father Hardin's radio show in which he addressed "God, Allah, Yahweh, Jesus, Great Spirit"—Father Hardin's customary way of being inclusive.[42] Among Father's close acquaintances were Muslims, Jews, Buddhists, and members of various Protestant denominations. He cultivated a friendship with W. D. Muhammad, who was awarded an honorary degree. Muslim meetings were held in Martin facilities and several Muslims were prominent staff members at Martin.

Similarly, Father Hardin was a friend of several rabbis and prominent Jewish businessman; Allen Wurzman, also the recipient of an honorary degree, was among the largest donors to Martin. Father and Sister Jane carefully developed Martin Center College as nondenominational, yet prayer was an important feature of meetings, events, and classes. In his own words, Father Hardin expressed his ecumenism: "If I had a magic wand, once a month, I would shut down all the churches in town, and we would have to go downtown and pray together to the one God. And they might get to liking it. And if they get to liking it, then maybe they would come to the realization this one God made all of us, to live in community and love one another. They would probably hang me from the nearest telephone pole, but I'd sure like to try it." At its core, Father Hardin argued, is the basic value espoused by religions: "I don't think the Lord is going to divide the Catholics and Protestants. He's going to ask you, 'Did you love Me and did you love my neighbor?' He's going to ask that."[43]

Among the many positive attributes ascribed to Father Hardin, his vision is cited most frequently. He was clearly the "idea person" behind the programs at the Martin Center and Martin University. As a visionary, he relied on the skills and energy of Sister Jane to implement the ideas. The ideas flowed constantly. Whether superimposing a globe on the plan for the Martin education center, naming its hall the "Gathertorium," or using extremely innovative teaching techniques, Father Hardin's creativity was always on display.

At the end of his life, Father Hardin began to refer to himself as a prophet. He talked about broad issues, such as the environment, world peace, and future civilization. Martin alumnus Bernard McFarland saw this quality in Father Hardin and connected it to Father Hardin's drive and passion: "When you speak of prophet, they pretty much give and they are not driven by what

Father Hardin's gravestone, Saint Meinrad Cemetery.

men say, they're driven by doing what God has called them to do and I believe truly that he was a great man that had a prophetic word given to him and if he wasn't, we wouldn't be sitting here [at Martin University] today."[44]

Father Hardin's drive in pursuing his vision was legendary. Whether the idea involved enlisting help, developing a program, opposing something, or erecting a building, he was resolute on action: "My theory is that we'll always have problems, but that we have to keep working and we don't give up. Focus on what you can do—whether it be education or health or a combination. Just don't give up."[45] He practiced this philosophy as problems came his way and coached others to join him. Marty Greenan said, "Once he got his mind fixed on something, there was no way you could stop him. You couldn't change it, he was gone."[46] Sease agreed, "One of [Father Hardin's] characteristics obviously was stubbornness. He didn't ever take no for an answer. . . . He and Sister Jane were like a team of strong horses that were pulling a carriage that was heavier than they could carry, but they never gave up, they just plowed on as though the goal was there and they were going to make the goal."[47] Sease further indicated that Father Hardin's single-minded commitment and drive precluded interest in compromise or hearing any other opinion: "Boniface didn't want to be challenged much. The gracious person he was, he had his own opinion about how the place ought to be run and he didn't like the folks who challenged him."[48]

In addition to his vision for education to end racism, to heal, and to create servant-leaders, Father Hardin translated experience with health issues into action for change. Several of these initiatives were prompted by his own experience with smoking, prostate cancer, and diabetes, but he was also interested in addressing sickle-cell anemia, breast cancer, and other common problems in the black community. Often, when serving as an invited speaker, he would switch topics to promote awareness of one or more of these health issues. Toward the end of his life, he was especially focused on abused or neglected children, a topic that he did not live long enough to address programmatically.

An issue that was interwoven in talks and initiatives with which Father Hardin was connected was his concern for the earth. Reverence for the physical planet was connected in his mind with love of humanity across the earth. He said, "You have to be reconciled not only to people but to the land and to the sky and to creatures and animals. We have to be reconciled to all these things. We have become oppressors of the Earth at every level of life. I'm going to teach love. I'm going to teach people to love."[49] In his keynote speech at a meeting on "The Impact of Climate Change in Indiana," sponsored by a group called Sustainable Indiana 2016, Father Hardin said, "We are at that point in our life history. The earth is in our soul (energy), our mind, our heart. We must become climate changers, or die."[50]

More broadly Father Hardin was focused on healing, not only healing of the physical body and the earth, but also of the very qualities and actions that create dissonance and lead to divisions among people. "All across the world we learned to hurt one another. We have to learn to heal," he said. "Healing has become a passion with me, whether it's about cancer or whatever. I talk about prostate. I talk about breast cancer. I talk about pap smears for women. . . . But the healing of the nation, and the healing of the world, I think we are going to have to believe that we need to be healed all of us. . . . Healing is the positive thing. Whether it's anger or self-will, whatever it is. Because if we have pride, we need to be healed, and we have to pray for that."[51]

Father Hardin's humble upbringing and his vow of poverty gave him empathy for those in need, and he frequently made decisions from the heart rather than according to administrative protocol. He would apologize to individuals who came to his door asking for funds, saddened that he only had ten dollars in the house to give them. His friends and associates commented on his compassion:

- [Boniface was] very humble and very proud. Very proud, very humble. And very conscious of the poor people. One of his favorite characterizations was of the poor among us. And he was always very conscious of the poor among us. In fact, I would say that if he was asked to name some mission in life, it probably would have been to improve the lot of the poor. And he spent his life or his adolescent and adult life looking for ways to do that.[52]
- And I think that the legacy that he leaves behind is a bleeding heart, not only for African American people, but for people of poverty, people of illness. He hurt for other people's pain, whether it was financial, or marital, or whatever the problem. I think the burdens that he carried internally were for the aches that people had, the hurt, and I think his final hurt was for what he saw happening to Martin, because while he had years of its ascension, he could see that his dream was being shattered.[53]
- He was too much of a philanthropist. I loved him for it. If you needed something he would, personally if you needed anything, if he had any-

thing, he would give it to you. If you needed—if your lights were cut off—he would find a way to get your lights on if he knew about it and you asked him. And he didn't have a lot of resources.[54]

- Well, he was always kind of a conscience. He understood what poverty is because in a lot of ways he lived like a pauper. He didn't have a lot of money and so he understood what it was like for people to not have anything and he understood that it was not always their fault. He was not judgmental. So when people would stand up and be judgmental or seem to be judgmental about the poor, or about minorities, or about women, or about anybody else, he would always tend to bring it back home and say, "Look, here's the way it really is, here's what people have to do to really live. You may not know this but this is how it works."[55]

Those who knew Father Hardin frequently pointed out that he was the consummate educator. Taking a walk with him, remarked Mynelle Gardner, was an experience in learning: "Everything in the world just interested him. And you could learn so much from him. Don't go for a walk with him because that was a whole lesson in itself. Because he would start talking about what they put on the grass, and what they did with other things, there was just so much that he had in him, he'd be willing to share. He was always teaching, he was always teaching you something. Until sometimes you just said, 'Father, wait a minute, I can't absorb any more.'"[56]

One of Father Hardin's most remarkable intellectual assets was his proclivity for languages. As a youth, he easily parroted the Latin in the Mass rituals of the time, understanding the meaning as well as being able to replicate the sounds. In seminary he mastered German and Greek, as well as increasing his prowess with Latin. After his ordination, languages became a pastime with Father Hardin. He wanted very much to be able to converse with others in their native language. His friendship with the Sons of Norway organization led him to add Norwegian to his repertoire of over twelve languages.

Father Hardin's intellectual curiosity showed itself in his love for philosophy, astronomy, literature, music, and the arts. His personal library was extremely eclectic, demonstrating wide interests and passions. He conversed freely about classical concepts and quantum theory alike. His preaching and classroom explanations often involved word origins or diagrams as visual representations of his ideas. Yet, in all these aspects, he appeared humble and tailored his explanations to the level of the audience.

The most tangible accomplishment of Father Hardin is clearly found in Martin University—the idea, the physical campus, and the graduates. Other impacts date from his earlier days. As a young student and seminarian at Saint Meinrad Archabbey, he fostered racial inclusion by his very presence and success. His persistence in achieving admission and navigating the coursework and procedures involved in becoming a monk and ordained priest created an important precedent for the monastery and his fellow monks. He opened up possibilities for future African American candidates and reinforced the newfound commitment to diversity at the archabbey.

As a young priest who traveled to Indianapolis and other parts of Indiana and Kentucky to offer Mass and to recruit others to religious life, Father Hardin provided an inspiring role model for young Catholics and fostered optimism in African American Catholics that there was room for them in the Church. Through his fiery activism as associate pastor at Holy Angels, he brought to the forefront important issues such as racist police practices, school inequality, harmful highway disruption of neighborhoods, and lack of inclusion within the Catholic Church.

During the Martin Center years, Father Hardin and Sister Jane educated civic leaders and their community members on matters of racial pride, identity, and history, creating important communication tools, such as the *Afro-American Journal* and radio and television shows that helped African Americans and the white community alike to learn the truth about the illustrious accomplishments of Africans and African Americans. They opened the eyes of corporate America, school system teachers and officials, public employees and others to the ways in which racial bias was impeding social justice for all. They educated the community about sickle-cell anemia, and with Doctor Raymond Pierce and others, created a model program for doing so that was replicated throughout the country.

In struggling to create Martin University, Father Hardin and Sister Jane again developed a philosophy and educational approach that influenced many other institutions, particularly in its approach to adult learning. The impact that attending Martin University had on its thousands of graduates, however, is perhaps the legacy that stands paramount in considering the work of Father Hardin and Sister Jane. The many prominent public officials, teachers, religious leaders, and social-justice advocates educated at Martin have enriched the Indianapolis community and created a sense of empowerment within the black community.

MARTIN UNIVERSITY

Father Hardin and Sister Jane walking in Crown Hill Cemetery.

To a person, those who knew Father Hardin and Sister Jane characterized the motivation behind this extraordinary legacy as exceptionally altruistic. Fern (Snooks) Winger, sister of Sister Jane, said, "They brought everybody up to a higher level. They did it through compassion, and love, and just their sense of justice. They found so many innovative ways to make people better themselves, become better people. And I believe both of them lived entirely for their fellow man."[57] Gary Gibson, director of the Sickle Cell Center concurred, saying of Father Hardin: "It was absolutely clear that he believed in everything he did, and he believed it, at least apparently he believed it with all his heart, that whatever he did, he did it full bore and so in that you see this tremendous amount of passion, which as I said is really humanitarian driven; really wanting to help people; really seriously; really, really seriously wanting to help people and not for anything other than helping people; not for any kind of gain, not for any kind of notoriety, not for any kind of anything except knowing that he helped people, and that's I think remarkable."[58]

Through archival records and oral histories, it has been possible to document the life of a young boy, born in the tradition of "picking cotton on the way to church," who developed into a fiery fighter for social justice, and founded and provided thirty years of leadership for an institution of higher education. Father Boniface Hardin's life was remarkable for its drama, its warmth, and its integrity. His extraordinary passion, humility, and wisdom ran as a stream through his days. His influence crossed socioeconomic, racial, and occupational boundaries—he was widely known by people from all walks of life. His legacy includes not only a unique university, but also the positive changes he brought to the lives of its students, to the city of Indianapolis, to those he served as a priest, and to those he called friend. His story illustrates the power of vision, the vision that inspired Sister Jane Schilling to join with him and together, create a force for change that was powerful in its impact and wide in its scope. Only rarely do the values and characteristics of a person combine to enable conquest of the challenges of their circumstances to the extent that this man did. May the telling of his story hold his example high for others to remember and follow.

Afterword

The more I learn about Father Boniface Hardin the more fascinating, intriguing, and motivational he becomes. This book fills in many blanks and answers numerous questions I had about the legendary founder of Martin University. As the fourth president of this unique institution of higher education, I am indebted to his tremendous vision and accomplishment. I am truly challenged by his determination, tenacity, and courage to start a "second chance" college for nontraditional students in an urban neighborhood filled with barriers to academic success. The personal and intellectual stamina needed to make the vision a reality were anchored in a foundation of faith, prayer, and stubbornness unique to a small minority of leaders. His characteristics and successes drive my daily efforts of keeping his vision and legacy alive.

I met Father Hardin officially in December of 2007 when he presented me with an Honorary Doctorate of Humane Letters. However, I had observed him working within the community several years prior to that date. I knew he performed as Frederick Douglass and I knew he was highly respected in the community. I did not come to the city until July of 1990 and this was long after his years at Holy Angels and the Martin Center. He had moved the college to the Avondale Place location when I started to read about him in the *Indianapolis Recorder*. Being a graduate of a black university, Alabama A&M University, I was impressed with his ability to start a predominately black college in Indianapolis. I knew there was no other such school in Indiana. He presented a precious gift to this community and he seemed larger than life.

After his retirement I heard disturbing stories of the transition of leadership and of his exclusion from the university. Then, there were several other leadership changes and the common "word on the street" was that the university was struggling amid financial, governance, and leadership problems. After retiring as Superintendent of the Indianapolis Public Schools in February of 2013, my wife retired in June of 2013 and we started to pursue plans to return to the southeast part of the United States. However, after we returned from house hunting a group from Martin University approached me about being the interim president and I accepted the invitation in August of 2013 because I did not want to see Father Hardin's work and institution fail. I could not give up on his dream. The interim position turned into the full-time president in January 2014.

Father Hardin had Sister Jane Schilling to start and operate his school and I have been fortunate to put together a team, at the university, to right-size our academic programs, stabilize our financial operations, build a strong administrative leadership, upgrade and develop a strong institutional governance body, and increase efficiency and effectiveness of university operations. However, the greatest change was a move to reestablish a university culture and environment "like a family." This was the primary phrase used to describe the university under Father Hardin's and Sister Jane's leadership. It is currently used to capture the experience at the University. We are guided by three University Values:

Professionalism—In all personal interactions, products produced and University activities

Communication—Clear, appropriate, thoughtful, and intelligent

Support and Respect for All—People, relationships, citizenship, families, and social justice.

We want to empower, uplift, motivate, and inspire our students to change their lives and the futures of their families through education. In educating them we want them to remember the words of Father Hardin, "In this institution, which is nondenominational, we try to teach each other—the students, the faculty, the staff, that they ought to love each other. Now all the knowledge in the world and you don't have love and care for each other (is not what we are about). Because you can take knowledge and hurt people. But true love can't hurt anybody." Every day we are working to make "love" the guiding force behind our attitude and actions.

The other driving force behind Father Hardin's leadership and the legacy of the university was service to the community. This took the form of social justice, leadership, and outreach programs and activities. The vision of a "commu-niversity" is real and growing. Currently, we are in the early planning stage of creating a Martindale-Brightwood Education Zone. The university will anchor and facilitate a partnership and collaboration with other community agencies and organizations to provide a comprehensive support network of service for parent(s) and children from pregnancy through the end of grade five. The network will provide help and services for education, safety, security, and mental and physical health for children and families living in the boundaries of the Martindale-Brightwood Community (north boundary is Thirtieth Street, east boundary is North Sherman Drive, south boundary is Twenty-First Street to a line down to the Monon Trail, and the west boundary is the Monon Trail up to Thirtieth Street on the north). This initiative is scheduled to start in January of 2018. In the meantime, the university will continue to work with local churches for our after-school science program. The university will partner with churches, community groups and agencies for special programs and activities in the Father Hardin's Gathertorium.

The "Afterword" for Martin University and the vision and legacy of Father Hardin is "continuation." The vision is strong, the progress is expanding in all areas, the leadership is solid, the governance is professional, and the faculty and staff are positively building and expanding programs and activities. Martin University loves, educates, guides, and inspires students who need a unique place for learning. It is still "a family."

Doctor Eugene G. White
President Emeritus, Martin University

Appendix

An alphabetical list of those interviewed for the study of the life and work of Father Boniface Hardin. Tapes of the interviews are in the Boniface Hardin Collection, Indiana Historical Society William Henry Smith Memorial Library.

Blair, Charles: Former program evaluator with the Lilly Endowment from 1973 to 1986, part-time development staff and faculty member at Martin University for various periods; continued supporter.

Davis, Father Cyprian (deceased): First African American monk ordained at Saint Meinrad Archabbey, a nationally known scholar and teacher on black Catholicism. Received his undergraduate degree before entering, so did not know Father Hardin during his early days at the seminary but kept in touch with Father during his Indianapolis days and was a supporter.

Day, John (phone interview): Representative, Indiana House of Representatives, former colleague of Father Hardin on the Catholic Interracial Council and recipient of an honorary degree from Martin University.

Dillon, Priscilla: Former director of development at Martin University, 1996–2008.

Gardner, Mynelle: Assistant to Father Hardin and Sister Jane from the Holy Angels and Martin Center days. Later worked at Martin University in the president's office.

Gibson, Gary: Director of the Sickle Cell Center and board of trustees member at Martin University, 2005–8.

Gibson, John: Minister colleague who worked with Father Hardin on ecumenical and sustainability issues; shared office space during one period.

Glenn, Billie: Parishioner at Holy Angels Parish who was an early supporter and continued to have close ties with Father Hardin through his final illness.

Goens, Madie (interviewed with Margaret Smith): Indianapolis Public School teacher who worked with Father Hardin and Sister Jane to establish an education major at Martin University and taught in the program.

Greenan, Martin: Faculty member and former vice president for academic affairs at Martin University who held a variety of administrative roles beginning in 1989. Inspired by the Martin philosophy, he completed a dissertation on andragogy.

Hardin, Albert (joint interview with his brothers): Middle brother, able to provide information on family.

Hardin, Bill (joint interview with brothers, deceased): Oldest brother, closest in age before Father Hardin left home for seminary, and the best source to recount stories of Father's younger days.

Hardin, Doctor John (joint interview with his brothers, deceased): Youngest brother, whose role as a professor of history enabled him to provide context details.

Jelinski, Jane: Sister of Sister Jane Schilling, able to provide details on her life.

King, Doctor Derek: former professor of religion at Martin University and cousin of Doctor Martin Luther King Jr.

Kolentus, Father Bob (deceased): Faculty member and holder of various administrative positions at Martin University, former seminarian in Father Hardin's class at Saint Meinrad Archabbey, and an ordained priest.

Ladd, Clete: Alumnus of Martin University, former principal at Indianapolis area schools, past director of enrollment at Martin University.

Lundgren, Doctor Ralph (phone interview): Former program officer at the Lilly Endowment.

Mays, Bill (deceased): Director of Mays Chemical and philanthropist who supported Martin University.

McFarland, Bernard: Alumnus of Martin University and historian of Martindale-Brightwood Neighborhood, former recruiter at Martin University.

McKenna, Tom: Attorney, worked with Browning Investments and other firms, held public office, member of the board of trustees at Martin University, 1989–2007.

Moore, Jesse: Graduate of Martin University, in administrative roles with the state of Indiana and Purdue University, member of the board of trustees of Martin University from 2002 to 2012.

Nava, Usana: Former biology faculty member at Martin University.

Payne, Pat: Indianapolis Public School administrator and teacher, involved in program development at Martin University, and past participant in early Martin Center workshops.

Pierce, Doctor Raymond (deceased): Physician and cofounder of the Sickle Cell Anemia Center.

Quinn, Sister Pat: Teacher at Holy Angels School while Father Hardin and Sister Jane were there, past participant in early Martin Center workshops.

Riedman, Monsignor Joseph: Priest who had served at Holy Angels before Father Hardin and followed his career.

Saahir, Mikal: Alumnus of Martin University and Imam at Nur-Allah Islamic Center; continued supporter.

Schilling, Sister Jane (deceased): Sister of Saint Joseph of Carondolet and close associate of Father Boniface throughout his time in Indianapolis, in administrative roles at the Martin Center and founding vice president of Martin University.

Scott, David: Minister and associate of Father Hardin who assisted with radio broadcasts.

Sease, Doctor Gene: Former president of the University of Indianapolis, confidant of Father Hardin, now a principal with the Indianapolis management consulting and public relations firm of Sease, Gerig, and Associates serving Martin University; continued supporter.

Shaheed, Brenda: Alumna of Martin University who served in a number of administrative capacities, member of Martin University Board of Trustees.

Sherman, John: Former principal at Sherman and Company, the chief marketing firm employed by Martin University for many years; continued supporter.

Smith, Joe: Former parishioner at Holy Angels, attorney and public services administrator, now retired. Member of the Smith family that had a decades-long friendship with Father.

Smith, Margaret (joint interview with Madie Goens): Alumna and continued supporter of Martin University.

Staton, Liz (deceased): Former faculty member and administrator at Martin University.

Strong, Amanda: Parishioner at Holy Angels, former assistant to Father Hardin and Sister Jane.

Taylor, George: Former faculty member and member of administrative staff at Martin University.

Taylor, Father Kenneth (deceased): Pastor of Holy Angels Catholic Church and close associate of Father Hardin.

Tobin, Father Vincent (phone interview): Monk of Saint Meinrad Archabbey and former classmate of Father Hardin.

Treadwell, Doctor Pat: Physician and former parishioner of Holy Angels, former member of the board of directors of the Sickle Cell Center.

West, Bill: Vice president of Mays Chemical and former board of trustees member at Martin University, 1996–2008.

Westerhaus-Renfrow, Charlotte: Faculty member at Indiana University–Purdue University Indianapolis, former administrator at the National Collegiate Athletic Association and interim president of Martin University in 2011.

Winger, Fern (Snooks): Sister of Sister Jane Schilling, who maintained close contact with Sister Jane and Father Hardin over the years, supporter of Martin University.

Notes

Chapter 1

1. "Lifetime Achievement Awards: Father Boniface Hardin," *Indianapolis NUVO Weekly*, April 26, 2001.

2. The terms "black" and "white" will not be capitalized in keeping with the accepted style of historical manuscripts. However, when they appear capitalized in direct quotes, the capital letters will be preserved.

3. Father Hardin is called "Randy" when referring to the time before his ordination; after that, he is called "Father Hardin" except in direct quotes when others address him as "Father Boniface" or "Boniface."

4. Father Boniface Hardin, interview by Greg Stone, July 18, 1993, tape and typescript, 4, Indiana University Oral History Project, Bloomington, IN (hereafter cited as FBH Oral History).

5. Ibid. Although Father Hardin refers to his grandfather as a slave, he most likely meant his great-grandfather since his grandfather was born after Emancipation in 1872. See US 1890 Census.

6. Ben J. Webb, *The Centenary of Catholicism in Kentucky* (Lexington, KY: Charles Rogers, 1884); "The Kentucky Migration," http://freepages.genealogy .rootsweb.ancestry.com/~slhessick/peakes04.htm/.

7. Ivan E. McDougle, "Slavery in Kentucky, 1792–1865," *The Journal of Negro History* 3, no. 3 (July 1918), http://archive.org/stream/kentuckyslav ery00mcdo/kentuckyslavery00mcdo_djvu.txt/.

8. Father Boniface Hardin, "How Did I Get This Far?" speech to Indianapolis Rotary Club, February 13, 2001, typescript, 1, Father Boniface Hardin Collection, Indiana Historical Society William Henry Smith Memorial Library, Indianapolis (hereafter cited as Hardin Collection).

9. FBH Oral History, 5, 11; William Hardin, Albert Hardin, and John Hardin, interview with the author, Louisville, KY, July 27, 2013, digital tape and typescript, 9, Hardin Collection (hereafter cited as Hardin Brothers interview).

10. FBH Oral History, 6–7; Hardin Brothers interview, 1.

11. Hardin Brothers interview, 1.

12. FBH Oral History, 6.

13. Ibid., 17.

14. Peter Smith, "1819 Bardstown Church Honored," *Louisville Courier-Journal*, September 2, 2001.

15. Father Boniface Hardin, host, "Black Churches, Part 1," radio show, *The Afro American in Indiana*, OR 170, February 2, 1972, Archives of African American Music and Culture, Indiana University, https://media.dlib.indiana.edu/media_objects/7d278w89d/.

16. Hardin Brothers interview, 1–2.

17. Ibid., 2; Smith, "Bardstown," 4.

18. Hardin Brothers interview, 2.

19. Ibid., 3.

20. William Hardin, *The Call and the Life of Father Boniface Hardin*," play performed by the Christ the King Off-Broadway Players, Christ the King Church, Louisville, KY, October, 2012, DVD, in the possession of family of William Hardin.

21. "Smoketown: A Forgotten neighborhood," *Louisville Courier-Journal.* September 25, 1991.

22. Hardin Brothers interview, 2–3.

23. Ibid., 3.

24. Hardin, "How Did I Get This Far?" 1.

25. Hardin Brothers interview, 3.

26. FBH Oral History, 15.

27. Ibid., 18.

28. Ruth Holliday, "Founding Father: He's the Energy behind 'Community Need' College," *Indianapolis Star,* August 14, 1988.

29. Hardin Brothers interview, 3.

30. Ibid., 5–6.

31. Brother Dennis Newton, SVD, "Saint Augustine's Seminary," http://www.svdsouth.com/st.-augustine-seminary.html/.

32. Hardin Brothers interview, 6–7.

33. Ibid., 7.

34. Ibid.

35. Ibid.

36. "Saint Meinrad Archabbey," http://www.saintmeinrad.org/the-monastery/history/.

37. Father Cyprian Davis, interview with the author, October 11, 2013, Saint Meinrad, IN, digital tape and typescript, 2, Hardin Collection.

38. Davis interview, 1–2.

39. Ibid., 3; Robert Kolentus, "The Origins of Martin University, 1920–Present" (Indianapolis, unpublished, 2002), 1.

40. Hardin, "The Black Family, Part Two," *The Afro-American in Indiana*, OR 237, August 21, 1972, Archives of African American Music and Culture, IU, https://media.dlib.indiana.edu/media_objects/qv33s1124/.

41. Robert Kolentus, interview with the author, July 25, 2013, Indianapolis, digital tape and typescript, 2, Hardin Collection.

42. Father Vincent Tobin, telephone conversation with the author, July 9, 2014. Notes are available in the Hardin Collection.

43. Hardin, "Black Learning Processes," *The Afro-American in Indiana*, OR 216, March 20, 1973, Archives of African American Music and Culture, IU, https://media.dlib.indiana.edu/media_objects/08612r758/.

44. Hardin Brothers interview, 7; FBH Oral History, 21.

45. Davis interview, 2.

46. In their interviews, neither Tobin nor Kolentus recalled any discussion in the seminary about race.

47. Father Boniface Hardin, "Fettered Freedom—Russel H. Nye," term paper submitted at Saint Meinrad Seminary, sometime between 1954 and 1959, section is "My Opinion," 7, box 6, Hardin Collection.

48. Hardin, "Abe Lincoln, 31," *The Afro-American in Indiana*, OR 249, November 8, 1973, Archives of African American Music and Culture, IU, https://media.dlib.indiana.edu/media_objects/xg94hs83g/.

49. Tobin telephone conversation.

50. Ibid.

51. Hardin Brothers interview, 7.

52. Hardin, "Black Churches, Part 1."

53. Hardin Brothers interview, 8.

54. Hardin, "Black Learning Processes."

55. "Martin University continues to grow under Father Boniface Hardin's leadership," *Indianapolis Criterion*, October 26, 2001. The *Criterion* is the newspaper for the Archdiocese of Indianapolis.

56. Tobin telephone conversation.

57. Hardin, "How Did I Get This Far?" 2.

58. Father Boniface Hardin, document chronicling his duties after ordination, undated but all 1959 dates, Hardin Collection.

59. Untitled press release about Father Boniface Hardin ordination, Hardin Collection.

60. Father Bernard Strange letter to Right Reverend Bonaventure Knabel, April 8, 1958, Hardin Collection.

61. Hardin document of duties.

62. Davis interview, 2.

63. Hardin, "The Black Family, Part 2."

64. FBH Oral History, 32.

65. Ibid., 22.

Chapter 2

1. Ruth Holliday, "Founding Father: He's the Energy behind 'Community Need' College," *Indianapolis Star*, August 14, 1988.

2. Leonard Moore, "Ku Klux Klan," in *The Encyclopedia of Indianapolis*, edited by David J. Bodenhamer and Robert G. Barrows (Bloomington and Indianapolis: Indiana University Press, 1994), 879–92.

3. Linda Gugin and James Saint Clair, eds., *The Governors of Indiana* (Indianapolis: Indiana Historical Society Press, 2006), 265–66.

4. Todd Gould, *For Gold and Glory: Charlie Wiggins and the African American Racing Car Circuit* (Bloomington: Indiana University Press, 2002), 127–30.

5. Emma Lou Thornbrough, "The Turbulent Sixties," chapter 8, *Indiana Blacks in the Twentieth Century* (Bloomington: Indiana University Press, 2000).

6. The Polis Center Neighborhoods Project, "UNWA: United Northwest Area," http://polis.iupui.edu/RUC/Neighborhoods/UNWA/UNWANarrative.htm.

7. James V. Smith, Jr., "Creating Their Own Style from the White Tradition," *Indianapolis News*, September 18, 1986.

8. Ferdye Bryant, Margaret Graves, and Doris Parker, *A New Journey of Hope: Holy Angels Catholic Church, 1903–2003* (Indianapolis: Holy Angels Catholic Church, 2003), 13; Polis Center Neighborhoods Project, "UNWA."

9. Bryant, Graves, and Parker, *New Journey of Hope*, 13.

10. Ibid., 49, 51.

11. Ibid., 15.

12. Ibid.

13. Ibid., 16.

14. Joseph Smith, interview with the author, May 16, 2013, Indianapolis, digital tape and typescript, 3, Father Boniface Hardin Collection, Indiana Historical Society William Henry Smith Memorial Library, Indianapolis, IN (hereafter cited as Hardin Collection).

15. Bryant, Graves, and Parker, *New Journey of Hope*, 54; Stephen J. Ochs, *Desegregating the Altar* (Baton Rouge: Louisiana State University Press, 1990), 499.

16. Mynelle Gardner, interview with the author, May 29, 2013, Indianapolis, digital tape and typescript, 1, Hardin Collection.

17. Charles Blair, interview with the author, July 23, 2014, Indianapolis, digital tape and typescript, 1, ibid.

18. Father Cyprian Davis, interview with the author, Saint Meinrad, IN, October 11, 2013 digital tape and transcript, 8, ibid.

19. Smith interview, 5.

20. "Lifetime Achievement Awards," *Indianapolis NUVO,* April 26–May 3, 2001.

21. Father Boniface Hardin, interview with Greg Stone, July 18, 1993, tape and transcript, 63, IU Oral History Project, Bloomington, IN (hereafter cited as FBH Oral History).

22. Ibid.

23. Ibid., 64.

24. William Hardin, Albert Hardin, and John Hardin, interview with the author, Louisville, KY, July 20, 2013, digital tape and transcript, 10, Hardin Collection (hereafter cited as Hardin Brothers interview).

25. Smith interview, 5.

26. FBH Oral History, 59.

27. Sister Jane Schilling, interview with the author, April 23, 2013, Saint Louis, Hardin Collection, 3. Several others tell the same story, with slight variations, such as where the interaction took place and the exact words used.

28. Sister Jane's remarks, *Celebrating 30 Years of Educational Excellence at Martin University* (Indianapolis: Martin University, 2007), DVD.

29. Information on Sister Jane comes from interviews with her two sisters, Fern (Snooks) Winger and Jane Jelinski: Fern (Snooks) Winger, telephone interview with the author, October 31, 2014, digital tape and typescript, Hardin Collection; Jane Jelinski, written responses to interview questions from the author, November 9, 2014, ibid.

30. Although Fern Winger, and a Martin Center biography list Sister Jane's area of study as medieval history, the official record from the Sisters of Saint Joseph of Carondelet motherhouse lists it as ancient history, which is a subject more commonly taught in intermediate grades.

31. Stefanie Lee, discussion with the author, Indianapolis, July 18, 2015.

32. Winger interview, 3.

33. *Celebrating 30 Years Educational Excellence at Martin University*.

34. Winger telephone interview, 6.

35. Ibid., 16.

36. Amanda Strong, interview with the author, Indianapolis, December 2, 2013, digital tape and typescript, 9–10, Hardin Collection.

37. Thornbrough, *Indiana Blacks in the Twentieth Century*.

38. Ibid., Historian Richard Pierce attributes the lack of radicalism to the fact that African Americans had settled in Indiana early on through the presence of Underground Railroad routes in the state, increasing the African American population of Indianapolis earlier than in other cities. These settlers and their descendants thus saw Indianapolis as home, became accustomed to their condition, and were more inclined to fight for change within the system than to mobilize against it. Laws and arrangements that discriminated against them were disguised and procrastination and backroom tactics kept change from happening, creating a subtle, rather than blatant oppression. The resulting response from the African American community thus constituted a "polite protest" rather than the riots and angry demonstrations that occured elsewhere. Richard Pierce, *Polite Protest: The Political Economy of Race in Indianapolis, 1920–1970* (Bloomington: Indiana University Press, 2005).

39. Lawrence Lucas, *Black Priest, White Church: Catholics and Racism* (New York: Random House, 1970).

40. Hardin Brothers interview, 3.

41. FBH Oral History. Following the cited interview is an undated addendum written by Father Hardin that will be cited as FBH Oral History Addendum, 1.

42. Smith interview, 4.

43. Bryant, Graves, and Parker, *New Journey of Hope*, 34.

44. FBH Oral History Addendum, 1.

45. Smith interview, 19.

46. Father Boniface Hardin, interview with Alexander Jimenez and Ethan Ax (Indianapolis, 2006), videocassette, tape 3. Property of Martin University, Indianapolis.

47. Reverend Boniface Hardin and Committee Studying the Community, "The Holy Angels Study Report," mimeograph (Indianapolis: Holy Angels Catholic Church, October, 1966), Hardin Collection. The section on the Northwest Area Council is on an unnumbered appendix page. The mimeographed report was made public on October 12, 1966, "with the Mayor present."

48. "Minutes of the Meeting of the Committee Studying Our Community," December 27, 1966, Hardin Collection.

49. Father Boniface Hardin, "Letter of Boniface Hardin to William E. Schaefer," February 28, 1967, ibid.

50. Flanner House Move to the Northside Discussed," *Indianapolis Recorder,* February 3, 1967; "Council Criticizes Mayor Barton's Absence in Depressed Highway Move," *Indianapolis Recorder,* July 1, 1967.

51."Captains of Eight Teams," *Indianapolis Recorder,* June 18, 1966; "Mayor's Task Force to Study City's Low-Income Needs," *Indianapolis Recorder,* August 5, 1967; "CAAP Names Five for Board of Directors," *Indianapolis Recorder*, September 17, 1966; "Complete Dance Plans," *Indianapolis Recorder*, May 13, 1967; "Top Named Bands, Vocalists in 'Musical Showcase '67,'" *Indianapolis Recorder*, July 8, 1967.

52. Bryant, Graves, and Parker, *New Journey of Hope*, 14.

53. Smith interview, 3.

54. Remarks by Paul Washington Lacey at ceremony honoring Father Hardin, *Sankofa Awards* (University of Indianapolis, March 26, 2007), DVD.

55. Billie Glenn, interview with the author, June 3, 2013, Indianapolis, digital tape and typescript, 1, Hardin Collection.

56. As told by Sister Jane Schilling in Bryant, Graves, and Parker, *New Journey of Hope*, 36.

57. Clete Ladd, interview with the author, October 14, 2013, Indianapolis, digital tape and typescript, Hardin Collection

58. Gardner interview, 2.

59. Smith interview, 8.

60. Thornbrough, *Indiana Blacks in the Twentieth Century*, 175.

61. Monsignor Joseph Reidman, interview with the author, July 15, 2013, Indianapolis, digital tape and typescript, 2, Hardin Collection.

62. "Study Shows Feasible Group Explains," *Indianapolis Recorder*, July 15, 1967.

63. Smith interview, 3.

64. Sister Jane Schilling's remarks, *Celebrating 30 Years of Educational Excellence.*

65. "Study Shows"; Also, "Petition Urges Depressed Innerloop," *Indianapolis Recorder,* August 26, 1967.

66. "Parents Fearful for Children if Interstate Elevated," ibid., September 9, 1967.

67. "Gov. May Seek I-65 Change," ibid., October 14, 1967.

68. "Mayor Considers Depressing of Interstate 65," ibid., December 2, 1967.

69. Patricia Treadwell, interview with the author, July 2, 2013, Indianapolis, digital tape and typescript, Hardin Collection.

70. "CORE Threatens Protest in Planned Highway Controversy," *Indianapolis Recorder*, February 10, 1968.

71. "Seek Lawsuit to Halt Construction of Highway thru Negro Community," ibid., February 3, 1968.

72. Ibid.

73. "Militants, Students Arrested after Shortridge Protest Demonstration," *Indianapolis Recorder*, March 1, 1969.

74 "Establishment Seeks Priest's Ouster," ibid., March 29, 1969; Smith interview; Strong interview, 5.

75. Joseph Smith made this remark during a radio interview with several others, conducted by radio personality Amos Brown on *The Light*, the most influential radio program within the black community, at the time of Father Hardin's death. Amos Brown," Update: Father Boniface Hardin, Fighter for Justice, Founder Martin University, Dies," March 24, 2012, http://praiseindy .com/1567256/father-boniface-hardin-fighter-for-justice-founder-martin -university-dies/

76. Richard Lugar, letter to Father Boniface Hardin, April 14, 1969, Hardin Collection.

77. "Spokesman for Mayor Denies Ouster Attempt," *Indianapolis Recorder*, April 5, 1969.

78. Father Boniface Hardin, letter to Archabbot Gabriel Verkamp, March 26, 1969, Hardin Collection.

79. FBH Oral History Addendum, 44.

80. Davis interview, 3–4, 6–7.

81. Reverend Donald Clark, letter to Most Reverend Paul C. Schulte, undated (likely in spring of 1969), Hardin Collection.

82. Dr. Raymond Pierce, interview with the author, July 11, 2013, Indianapolis, digital tape and typescript, 6–7, ibid.

83. Father Hardin to Archabbot Verkamp.

84. Father Albert Ajamie, letter to Holy Angels parishioners, March 29, 1969, Hardin Collection.

85. FBH Oral History Addendum, 4.

86. Concerned Black Catholics, "In an effort to clarify issues. . .," statement addressed to Archbishop Paul Schulte, undated (likely in early spring of 1969), Hardin Collection.

87. Strong interview, 2.

88. Concerned Black Catholics, *Easter Sunday Statement,* released April 20, 1969, Hardin Collection.

89. "Demonstrators Protest Treatment of Priest," *Indianapolis Recorder,* April 12, 1969; "150 Walk Out in a Protest at Indianapolis Cathedral," *New York Times,* April 7, 1969. The incident was widely reported in a number of local papers. See, for example, *Anderson Daily Bulletin,* April 7, 1969; *Rushville Republican,* April 7, 1969; *Fresno (CA) Bee/Republican,* April 7, 1969; and *Lindon Daily Citizen,* April 7, 1969.

90. "Demonstrators Protest Treatment of Priest."

91. "Council Criticizes Mayor Barton's Absence in Depressed Highway Move."

92. Sister Jane Schilling in Bryant, Graves, and Parker, *New Journey of Hope,* 36.

93. "Indianapolis Priest Leads Death Protest," *Anderson Herald,* July 18, 1969.

94. FBH Oral History Project Addendum, 2.

95. Ibid.

96. Martin University, "Heritage Statement," August 30, 2005 (document likely prepared for the strategic plan being developed that year), Hardin Collection.

97. Ibid.

98. Gardner interview, 3.

99. Black Catholic Clergy Caucus, minutes, undated (likely, sometime in spring 1968), Hardin Collection

100. Black Catholic Clergy Caucus, "Statement on Black Catholics in the Church," April 18, 1968, Hardin Collection.

101. Reverend Rollins Lambert and Executive Committee of the Black Catholic Clergy Caucus, letter to Archbishop John Deardon, November 1968, ibid.

102. Unnamed Regional Group of the Black Catholic Clergy Caucus, minutes, January 2, 1969, ibid.

103. Black Catholic Clergy Caucus, *Newsletter,* undated (likely between mid-January and April, 1969), ibid.

104. Black Catholic Clergy Caucus, "Chairman's Report," April 24, 1969, ibid.

105. Black Catholic Clergy Caucus, minutes, New Orleans Meeting, April 24, 1969, and Black Catholic Clergy Caucus, "Agenda for National Meeting at Holy Spirit Retreat House," Techny, IL, November 25–29, 1968, ibid.

106. Father Boniface Hardin, "*The Central Office for Black Catholicism in the U.S.A.*," May 31, 1968, p. 1, ibid.

107. Ibid., 3.

108. Reverends Barnardin Patterson and Boniface Hardin, "*The Central Office of the National Black Catholic Clergy Caucus*," 2, undated (most likely in late spring, 1969), Hardin Collection.

109. Father Boniface Hardin, outline of talk for National Black Catholic Clergy Caucus, June 13, 1969, ibid.

110. Father Boniface Hardin, "The Church in Black Indianapolis," undated (likely in late August or early September, 1969), ibid.

111. Father Hardin, letter to Archabbot Verkamp, OSB, October 30, 1969, ibid.

112. Father Boniface Hardin, letter to Mr. Warren Atkinson, November 20, 1969, p. 1 ibid.

113. FBH Oral History Addendum, 5.

114. Father Kenneth Taylor, interview with the author, August 7, 2013, Indianapolis, digital tape and typescript, 8, Hardin Collection.

115. Father Boniface Hardin, letter to Most Rev. Harold Perry, December 31, 1969, p. 1, ibid.

116. Father Boniface Hardin, letter to Archbishop Paul Schulte, December 5, 1969, p. 1, ibid.

117. Father Hardin, letter to Archabbot Verkamp, OSB, December 13, 1969, p. 1, ibid.

118. Father Hardin, handwritten draft of letter to Archabbot Verkamp, undated (likely written before December 13, 1969), 1, ibid.

119. FBH Oral History, 44.

120. FBH Oral History Addendum, 4.

121. Father Boniface Hardin, "My Dear Friends," letter to parishioners of Holy Angels Church, December 31, 1969, p. 1, Hardin Collection.

122; "*Lifetime Achievement Awards.*"

Chapter 3

1. "In Depth," [*Indianapolis Star*] *Intake Weekly*, September 28, 2006.

2. Archabbot Gabriel Verkamp OSB, letter to Father Boniface Hardin, December 15, 1969, Father Boniface Hardin Collection, Indiana Historical

Society William Henry Smith Memorial Library, Indianapolis, IN (hereafter cited as Hardin Collection).

3. Joseph Smith, interview with the author, May 16, 2016, digital tape and transcript, 6, Hardin Collection.

4. Smith interview, 13.

5. Father Boniface Hardin, "My Dear Friends," letter to parishioners of Holy Angels Church, December 31, 1969, Hardin Collection.

6. Father Boniface Hardin, host, *The Afro American in Indiana* radio series, Number 48, OR 231, Archives of African American Music and Culture, Indiana University, https://media.dlib.indiana.edu/media_objects/k3569764p/.

7. Father Boniface Hardin, addendum to interview with Greg Stone, July 18, 1993, Indiana University Oral History Project, Bloomington, IN, 4 (hereafter cited as FBH Oral History Addendum).

8. Mikal Saahir, "A Man Everyone Needs to Know: Father Boniface Hardin, the President of Martin University in Indianapolis, IN," *Muslim Journal* (June 17, 2004): 2.

9. "St. Martin de Porres," Catholic Online, http://www.catholic.org/saints/saint.php?saint_id=306

10. Ethan Ax, "A Mission of Service, Rev. Father Boniface Hardin Founder of Martin University Retires" *The Black Collegian*, Second Semester Issue (2007).

11. Undated and unlabeled funding proposal for expansion of Martin Center, around 1973, Hardin Collection.

12. Martin University, "Heritage Statement," 205, Hardin Collection.

13. Father Boniface Hardin, interview with Greg Stone, July 18, 1993, p. 60, Indiana University Oral History Project, Bloomington, IN (hereafter cited as FBH Oral History).

14. Father Pat Doyle, telephone interview by the author, April 27, 2016, p. 1. Notes are in the Hardin Collection.

15. Smith interview, 15.

16. Sister Pat Quinn, CSJ, telephone interview with the author, April 29, 2015, digital tape and typescript, 4, Hardin Collection.

17. Sister Jane Schilling, letter to Sister Mary Ann Smith, CSJ, June 13, 1985, ibid.

18. Ibid.

19. Brochure quoted in Al McCreary, "'Relevant' Church Can Effect Changes," *Louisville Record*, October 1, 1970.

20. Bylaws of Martin Center Inc., May 22, 1970, Hardin Collection.

21. "Seed Money," *Martin Center Newsletter* 1, no. 1 (1970). Reproduced in the appendix of an untitled Martin Center grant proposal book, Hardin Collection.

22. Smith interview, 15.

23. Mynelle Gardner, interview with the author, May 29, 2003, Indianapolis, digital tape and transcript, 17, Hardin Collection.

24. "Progress becomes visible," *Martin Center Newsletter*.

25. "Ethnotherapy," draft of a funding proposal to unnamed organization, 1992, Hardin Collection.

26. Karen E. Johnson, "Martin Center College: A New Approach to Education," *Avenues* 2 (September–October 1982), 27.

27. Gardner interview, 4–5.

28. Ibid., 5.

29. Ibid., 6.

30. Doyle interview, 1.

31. Quinn interview, 7.

32. Pat Payne interview with the author, May 6, 2015, Indianapolis, Hardin Collection.

33. "City Chosen to Study Sickle Cell," [Martin Center] *Community Bulletin*, July 2–8, 1972, p. 2. Reproduced in the appendix of an untitled Martin Center grant proposal book, Hardin Collection.

34. Gardner interview, 17. Descriptions of the Afro-American Institute are also contained on the tapes of two radio broadcasts cohosted by Father Hardin and Sister Jane, numbers 175 and 202 in *The Afro American in Indiana* series, Archives of African American Music and Culture at Indiana University. Digitized versions of more than a hundred weekly radio shows are available through the archives. See, https://media.dlib.indiana.edu/?_=1498674773806 &f%Bcollection_ssim%5D%5B%5D=The+Afro-American+in+Indiana+%28rad io+series%29/.

35. "Martin Center's Success Is Vehicle by Father Boniface," *Indianapolis Recorder*, March 11, 1972.

36. Ibid.

37. "Proposal for expansion of Martin Center," 11, Hardin Collection.

38. Various versions of Father Hardin's curriculum vitae list these activities. For example, see "Father Boniface Hardin," Spirit and Place Festival website, 2007, http://www.spiritandplace.org/PastFestivals.aspx?access=Peop

le&Year=2007&PeopleID=225. Father Hardin also spoke of these activities in FBH Oral History, 41.

39. "The Afro-American in Indiana," *Indianapolis Recorder,* November 11, 1972.

40. FBH Oral History, 41. Collections of the *Afro American Journal* are in the Indiana University libraries, the Indiana State Library, the Indianapolis–Marion County Public Library, and the Hardin Collection.

41. William L. Van DeBurg, *New Day in Babylon: The Black Power Movement and American Culture, 1965–1975* (Chicago: University of Chicago Press, 1992).

42. *Afro-American Journal* 1, no. 2 (1973): 1.

43. Both films are available in their original Betamax format and DVD, Hardin Collection.

44. Boniface Hardin, "The Effects on the Self-Image of the Afro-American and the Perpetuation of Racism in the Dissemination of Historical Studies by the Communication Media," *Afro-American Journal* 2, no. 8 (Nov.–Dec. 1974): 19. Father Hardin also included the poem in a speech delivered at the annual convention of the Association for the Study of Afro-American Life and History, Philadelphia, October 24, 1974.

45. Gardner interview, 8.

46. FBH Oral History Addendum, 5.

47. Fern (Snooks) Winger, telephone interview with the author, October 31, 2014, digital tape and transcripts, 8, Hardin Collection.

48. Sister Jane Schilling, interview with the author April 25, 2015, Saint Louis, digital tape and transcript, 5, ibid.

49. Ibid., 8.

50. Payne interview, 2.

51. "Proposal for expansion of Martin Center," Hardin Collection.

52. Gardner interview, 9.

53. Martin University, "Heritage Statement," 2.

54. PatriciaTreadwell, interview with the author, July 2, 2013, Indianapolis, digital type and transcript, 6, Hardin Collection.

55. Charmaine R. Bissell, "Black Priest Combines Church with Making Social Reforms," *Indianapolis Recorder,* June 22, 1974, p. 3.

56. Sister Jane Schilling, in, *Celebrating 30 Years of Educational Excellence at Martin University* (Martin University, Indianapolis, 2007), DVD.

57. Sister Jane Schilling interview, 4.

Chapter 4

1. Ethan Ax, "A Mission of Service, Rev. Father Boniface Hardin Founder of Martin University Retires," *The Black Collegian*, Second Semester Issue (2007).

2. Father Boniface Hardin, interview with Alexander Jiminez and Ethan Ax, Indianapolis, 2006, videocassette, tape 3, Martin University.

3. "Martin University Book of Achievements, 1977–2004" (Indianapolis: Martin University), 4.

4. Mikal Saahir, "A Man Everyone Needs to Know: Father Boniface Hardin, the President of Martin University, Indianapolis, IN," *Muslim Journal* (June 17, 2004): 2.

5. Ibid.

6. Father Boniface Hardin, Notes for Founder's Day speech, April 20, 1992, p. 21, Father Boniface Hardin Collection, Indiana Historical Society William Henry Smith Memorial Library, Indianapolis, IN (hereafter cited as Hardin Collection).

7. Charles Blair, interview with the author, July 24, 2014, Indianapolis, digital tape and transcript, 2, Hardin Collection.

8. "Martin University Book of Achievements,"5.

9. Sister Jane Shilling, interview with the author, April 25, 2015, Saint Louis, tape and digital transcript, 10, Hardin Collection.

10. "The Founding of Martin Center College" *Martin Center College Catalog, 1980–82*, 3; "The Afro-American in Indiana," *Indianapolis Recorder*, November 11, 1972; "Registration now open for new course at Martin Center," *Indianapolis Recorder*, January 13, 1973.

11."In-Depth," [*Indianapolis Star] Intake Weekly*, September 28, 2006.

12. Mynelle Gardner, interview with the author, May 29, 2003, Indianapolis, digital tape and transcript, 10, Hardin Collection.

13. John Sherman, interview with the author, October 9, 2013, Indianapolis, digital tape and transcript, 1–2, ibid.

14."The Afro-American in Indiana"; "Registration Now Open for New Course at Martin Center."

15. "The Founding of Martin Center College."

16. "Heritage Statement"; "Martin University Book of Achievements," 10.

17. *Martin Center College Self-Study Report: January 1990 North Central Association of Colleges and Schools* (Indianapolis: Martin University, 1990), 4.

18. Malcolm Knowles, "Instructional Design: Theories—Andragogy (Malcolm Knowles)" *Encyclopedia of Psychology*, http://www.instructionaldesign.org/theories/andragogy.html.

19. "Andragogy," undated paper, no author cited, possibly Sister Jane's notes, from early 1990s, Hardin Collection.

20. Father Boniface Hardin, Notes on remarks as part of the Presidents' Panel, Leadership Summit, Indiana Humanities Council, November 1, 2001, p. 2, ibid.

21. Father Boniface Hardin, interview with Greg Stone, July 18, 1993, tape and typescript, p. 31, Indiana University Oral History Project, Bloomington, IN (hereafter cited as FBH Oral History).

22. "Martin University Book of Achievements," 14.

23. *Martin College Catalog*, 1980–82, p. 3.

24. Hardin, "Notes for Founder's Day."

25. Fact Sheet on Martin Center College (no date, but from Avondale address, possibly 1990), refers to seven students but the "Martin University Book of Achievements," 27, indicates that five students started.

26. Notes from the Legacy Meeting, which seems to have been a class project, April 8, 2002, group 1, Hardin Collection.

27. FBH Oral History, 31.

28. Norris Milton Archer, "The Founding of Martin University," 13, Hardin Collection.

29. "Martin University Book of Achievements," 13, 23, 27, 33.

30. Ibid., 10.

31. Judith Cebula, "A World of Difference," *Indianapolis Star,* July 14, 2001, F4.

32. Blair interview, 4.

33. Brian Steuerwald, e-mail message to author, June 15, 2015.

34. Untitled enrollment brochure (1984), Hardin Collection.

35. "Martin Center College Self-Study Report," appendix B.

36. "Martin University Book of Achievements," 12.

37. Liz Staton, interview with the author, June 6, 2013, digital tape and transcript, 1, 4, Hardin Collection.

38. Martin Center College Board of Trustees meeting minutes, July 10, 1984.

39. Robert Kolentus, interview, with the author, July 25, 2013, Indianapolis, digital tape and transcript, 4–5, Hardin Collection.

40. Thomas McKenna, interview with the author, November 10, 2014, Indianapolis, digital tape and transcript, 2, Hardin Collection.

41. Kolentus interview, 5.

42. Sister Jane Schilling, remarks at retirement dinner, *Celebrating 30 Years of Educational Excellence at Martin University* (Indianapolis: Martin University, 2007), DVD, Hardin Collection.

43. "Open House to Celebrate Martin College Milestones," *Indianapolis Recorder*, June 6, 1987, p. 20.

44. "Martin University Book of Achievements," 20.

45. Gardner interview, 9.

46. "Martin University Book of Achievements," 20.

47. Priscilla Dillon, interview with the author, July 10, 2014, Indianapolis, digital tape and transcript, 3, Hardin Collection.

48. Ibid.

49. Malcolm Knowles, letters to Sister Jane Schilling, October 21, 1993, November 20, 1993, Hardin Collection.

50. *Martin Center College Catalog*, 1989–91, p. 3.

51. Jennifer Wagner, "College Diplomas Symbolize New Beginnings for Inmates," *Indianapolis Star*, May 12, 2001, pp. 1–5; "A Troubled Life Is Restored Behind Bars," Staff editorial, *Indianapolis Star*, May 13, 2001, pp. 16, 10.

52. Jane Ann Lemon, "Privately funded classes for inmates," *Indianapolis Star*, May 23, 2001

53. FBH Oral History, 40.

54. "Martin University Book of Achievements," 42–43.

55. *Annual Report, Martin University, 2003–04* (Indianapolis: Martin University, 2005), 6.

56. "Martin University Book of Achievements," 39.

57. "Humane Exchange," brochure, Martin University, no date (possibly around 1997, since it is described as a new program), Hardin Collection.

58. Father Boniface Hardin, handwritten diagram for Centre for Humane Exchange, no date (possibly around 1997), ibid.

59. Martin Greenan, interview with the author, November 19, 2014, digital tape and transcript, 1, ibid.

60. Father Boniface Hardin, notes for speech on dedication of new education center, October 13, 2001, p. 2, Hardin Collection.

61. Mikal Saahir, interview, 2.

62. Clete Ladd, interview with the author, October 14, 2013, Indianapolis, digital tape and transcript, 1, Hardin Collection; Mikal Saahir, interview with the author, August 9, 2013, digital tape and transcript, 2, ibid.

63. Gardner interview, addendum, 1.

64. "Martin University Book of Achievements," 29.

65. "Martin News Pictorial" (Indianapolis: Martin University, 2000), 3.

66. Greenan interview, 4.

67. "Martin University Book of Achievements," 35.

68. Margaret Nelson, "Awards Bring Attention to Education as Ministry," *Criterion* (newspaper of the Archdiocese of Indianapolis), August 25, 1995, p. 3.

69. Brenda Shaheed, interview with the author, September 5, 2013, Indianapolis, digital tape and typescript, 2, 4, Hardin Collection.

70. "In-Depth," 25.

71. Ladd interview, 5–6.

72. Gardner interview, 6.

73. Ladd interview, 5.

74. Ibid., 2.

75. Margaret Smith and Madie Goens, interview with the author, July 16, 2013, Indianapolis, digital tape and transcript, 1–2, Hardin Collection.

76. Ladd interview, 1.

77. FBH Oral History, 58.

78. Ibid., 46.

79. "Blessing of I-70 Road and Railroad Tracks and Builders, no date (most likely in 2007 when the highway was elevated along the Martin property line), Hardin Collection.

80. 2014 Self-Study Report Submitted to the Higher Learning Commission of the North Central Association of Colleges and Schools (Indianapolis: Martin University, July 2014), 35.

81. Saahir, "A Man Everyone Needs to Know, 3.

82. Meghan McCormick, "Douglass Double Take," *Indianapolis Monthly* 24 (March 2001): 58.

83. Nelson, "Awards Bring Attention," 3.

84. Gardner interview, 10.

85. Father Boniface Hardin, Program for "An Anti-Slavery Meeting at Pendleton, Indiana" (Indianapolis: Martin University, March 20, 1999).

86. Blair interview, 6.

87. William Mays, interview with the author, October 16, 2013, Indianapolis, digital tape and typescript, 8, Hardin Collection.

88. "Executive Compensation," *The Chronicle of Higher Education* (November 24, 2006), http://onlineathens.com/multimedia/news/06college_pres_salaries/colpressal.pdf.

89. Blair interview, 12.

90. Gary Quehl, "Review of the Martin University Advancement Program: Professional Standards, Current Achievements, Recommended Actions" (Nevada City, CA, Quehl Associates, 2005), 19.

91. Greenan interview, 5.

92. Blair interview, 7.

93. Greenan interview, 4.

94. Shaheed interview, 9.

95. Greenan interview, 3.

96. Ibid, 4.

97. Ibid.

98. Blair interview, 8.

99. McKenna interview, 6.

100. Blair interview, 10.

101. Bernard McFarland, interview with the author, June 22, 2015, Indianapolis, digital tape and typescript, 7, Hardin Collection.

102. Bill West, interview with the author, October 21, 2013, Indianapolis, digital tape and typescript, 7, ibid.

103. Ibid.

104. Gene Sease, interview with the author, November 4, 2013, Indianapolis, digital tape and typescript, 2, Hardin Collection.

105. Gary Gibson, interview with the author, July 11, 2013, Indianapolis, digital tape and typescript, 4, ibid.

106. Martin University Strategic Plan, ibid.

107. Saahir, "A Man Everyone Needs to Know," 6.

108. Father Boniface Hardin, remarks at retirement dinner, *Celebrating 30 Years of Educational Excellence at Martin University*.

Chapter 5

1. Ethan Ax, "A mission of Service: Father Boniface Hardin of Martin University Retires," *Black Collegian*, second semester issue (2007):77.

2. Commitment by Martin University to Father Boniface Hardin and Sister Jane Schilling, December 31, 2007, Father Boniface Hardin Collection, Indiana Historical Society William Henry Smith Memorial Library, Indianapolis (hereafter cited as Hardin Collection). The agreement is signed by Father Hardin and Sister Jane and Jim Scott, vice president for finance, and John Goss, chairman of the board of trustees finance committee.

3. Brandon Perry, "Hardin to Still Be Force in Community," *Indianapolis Recorder*, November 23, 2007, A1-3.

4. Father Boniface Hardin, "Hagia Sophia," handwritten document, May 9, 2010, p. 1. This document explains how the symbol of Hagia Sophia is used in what appears to be an earlier undated document.

5. In a 2004 interview with Mikal Saahir, Father Hardin said that he had some knowledge of seventeen languages. Mikal Saahir, "A Man Everyone Needs to Know: Father Boniface Hardin, the President of Martin University in Indianapolis, IN" *Muslim Journal* (June 17, 2004): 5.

6. Father Boniface Hardin, "Sophia [written in Greek letters]," undated document, probably written in 2009.

7. Sources that document the changes during the Freeman years include: "Controversial Martin University President Draws Ire," *Indiana Business Journal*, July 21, 2008; "Martin University President Algeania Freeman to Step Down after Three Years on the Job," *Indiana Business Journal*, December 7, 2010; "Controversial Martin University President to Retire This Month," *Indiana Business Journal*, December 6, 2010; "Martin U President Steps Down," *Indianapolis Recorder*, December 10, 2010; Shannon Williams, "There's No Middle Ground with Algeania Freeman," *Indianapolis Recorder*, December 10, 2010.

8. Hardin, "Sophia."

9. Billie Glenn, interview with the author, June 2, 2013, Indianapolis, digital tape and transcript, 3, Hardin Collection.

10. Charles Blair, interview with the author, July 13, 2014, Indianapolis, digital tape and transcript, 11, ibid.

11. Boniface Hardin, "Planning My Life," 2, handwritten document, April 5, 2008, Hardin Collection.

12. Sister Jane Shilling, interview with the author, Saint Louis, April 23, 2013, digital tape and transcript, 16, Hardin Collection.

13. John Gibson, interview with the author, September 30, 2013, digital tape and typescript, 2, Hardin Collection.

14. Hardin, "Planning My Life," 9.

15. Blair interview, 9.

16. "Controversial Martin University President to Retire This Month"; "Martin U President Steps Down."

17. Charlotte Westerhaus-Renfrow, interview with the author, September 12, 2013, Indianapolis, digital tape and typescript, 1, Hardin Collection.

18. Ibid., 2.

19. Ibid., 3.

20. Recollections of Stefanie Lee, who served as caregiver to Father Hardin and Sister Jane during their retirement. Stephanie Lee, discussion with the author, July 18, 2015, Indianapolis, Hardin Collection.

21. Westerhaus-Renfrow interview, 3.

22. Schilling interview, 18.

23. Gary Gibson, interview with the author, July 11, 2013, digital tape and typescript, 3, Hardin Collection.

24. Mynelle Gardner, interview with the author, May 29, 2013, digital tape and transcript, 15, ibid.

25. John Day, telephone interview with the author, September 25, 2013, p. 1, notes available, ibid.

26. The author was the professor in this classroom and witnessed the event.

27. Father Boniface Hardin, interview with Alexander Jiminez and Ethan Ax, Indianapolis, 2006, videocassette tapes, Martin University.

28. Margaret Nelson, "Awards Bring Attention to Education as Ministry," *Indianapolis Criterion*, August 25, 1995, p. 3.

29. Gene Sease, interview with the author, November 4, 2013, digital tape and transcript, 4, Hardin Collection.

30. Ibid., 2.

31. Blair interview, 12–13.

32. Glenn interview, 1.

33. Blair interview, 8.

34. Father Boniface Hardin, interview with Greg Stone, July 18, 1993, tape and typescript, Addendum, 3, Indiana University Oral History Project, Bloomington (hereafter cited as FBH Oral History Addendum).

35. Father Boniface Hardin, interview with Greg Stone, July 18. 1993, tape and typescript, 45, Indiana University Oral History Project, Bloomington.

36. FBH Oral History Addendum, 6.

37. Ibid.

38. Judith Cebula, "A World of Difference," *Indianapolis* Star, July 14, 2001, F4.

39. FBH Oral History Addendum, 6.

40. "'Relevant' Church Can Effect Changes."

41. Saahir, "A Man Everyone Needs to Know," 6.

42. Mikal Saahir, interview with the author, August 9, 2013, Indianapolis, digital tape and transcript, 1, Hardin Collection.

43. FBH Oral History Addendum, 47.

44. Bernard McFarland, interview with the author, June 22, 2015, Indianapolis, digital tape and transcript, 4, Hardin Collection.

45. "Lifetime Achievement Awards," *Indianapolis* NUVO, April 26–May 3, 2001, p. 29.

46. Martin Greenan, interview with the author, November 19, 2014, Indianapolis, 2, Hardin Collection.

47. Sease interview, 6.

48. Ibid., 5.

49. Bonnie Harris, "Award Honors Global Vision," *Indianapolis Star*, September 14, 2002.

50. *"The Impact of Climate Change in Indiana, 2008,"* (Sustainable Indiana 2016), DVD, Hardin Collection.

51. Saahir, "A Man Everyone Needs to Know," 3.

52. Bill West, interview with the author, October 21, 2013, Indianapolis, digital tape and transcript, 1, Hardin Collection.

53. Sease interview, 6.

54. Blair interview, 7.

55. Ibid., 7–8.

56. Gardner interview, 7.

57. Fern (Snooks) Winger, telephone interview with the author, October 31, 2014, digital tape and typescript, 18, Hardin Collection.

58. Gibson interview, 6.

Bibliography

Special Collections

Hardin, Father Boniface, Collection. Indiana Historical Society William Henry Smith Memorial Library, Indianapolis, IN.

Hardin, Father Boniface. Interview by Greg Stone, July 18, 1993. Tape and typescript. Indiana University Oral History Project. Lilly Library, Bloomington, IN.

Indianapolis Recorder Collection. Indiana Historical Society William Henry Smith Memorial Library, Indianapolis, IN.

Books

Gould, Todd. *For Gold and Glory: Charlie Wiggins and the African American Racing Car Circuit*. Bloomington, IN: Indiana University Press, 2002.

Bryant, Ferdye, Margaret Graves, and Doris Parker. *A New Journey of Hope: Holy Angels Catholic Church, 1903–2003*. Indianapolis: Holy Angels Catholic Church, 2003.

Gugin, Linda, and James Saint Clair, eds. *The Governors of Indiana*. Indianapolis: Indiana Historical Society Press, 2006.

Knowles, Malcolm. "Instructional Design: Theories—Andragogy (Malcolm Knowles)." In *Encyclopedia of Psychology*. http://www.instructionaldesign.org/theories/andragogy.html

Lucas, Lawrence. *Black Priest, White Church: Catholics and Racism*. New York: Random House, 1970.

Moore, Leonard. "Ku Klux Klan." In *The Encyclopedia of Indianapolis*. Edited by David J. Bodenhamer and Robert G. Barrows. Bloomington and Indianapolis: Indiana University Press, 1994.

Pierce, Richard. *Polite Protest: The Political Economy of Race in Indianapolis, 1920–1990*. Bloomington: Indiana Univeristy Press, 2005.

Thornbrough, Emma Lou. *Indiana Blacks in the Twentieth Century*. Bloomington: Indiana University Press, 2000.

Van DeBurg, William L. *New Day in Babylon: The Black Power Movement and American Culture, 1965–1975*. Chicago: University of Chicago Press, 1992.

Webb, Ben. J. *The Centenary of Catholicism in Kentucky*. Lexington, KY: Charles Rogers, 1884.

Periodicals

Afro-American Journal 1, no. 2 (1973).

Ax, Ethan. "A Mission of Service, Rev. Father Boniface Hardin Founder of Martin University Retires." *The Black Collegian*. Second Semester Issue (2007).

McDougle, Ivan E. "Slavery in Kentucky, 1792–1865." *The Journal of Negro History* 3, no. 3 (July, 1918). http://archive.org/stream/kentuckyslavery00mcdo/kentuckyslavery00mcdo_djvu.txt

Saahir, Mikal. "A Man Everyone Needs to Know: Father Boniface Hardin, the President of Martin University in Indianapolis, IN." *Muslim Journal* (June 17, 2004).

Newspapers

Anderson Herald.
Indiana Business Journal.
Indianapolis Criterion.
Indianapolis News.
Indianapolis NUVO Newsweekly.
Indianapolis Star.
Indianapolis Recorder.
Louisville Courier-Journal.
Louisville Record.
New York Times.

Websites

Brown, Amos."Update: Father Boniface Hardin, Fighter for Justice, Founder Martin University, Dies." http://praiseindy.com/1567256/father-boniface-hardin-fighter-for-justice-founder-martin-university-dies/.

"Father Boniface Hardin." Spirit and Place Festival. 2007. http://www.spiritandplace.org/PastFestivals.aspx?access=People&Year=2007&PeopleID=225.

"The Kentucky Migration Rootsweb, an Ancestry.com Community. http://freepages.genealogy.rootsweb.ancestry.com/~slhessick/peakes04.htm.

Newton Dennis, SVD. "Saint Augustine's Seminary." http://www.svdsouth.com/st.-augustine-seminary.html.

"The Polis Center Neighborhoods Project, "UNWA: United Northwest Area." Polis Center. http://polis.iupui.edu/RUC/Neighborhoods/UNWA/UNWANarrative.htm.

"Saint Meinrad Archabbey." http://www.saintmeinrad.org/the-monastery/history/.

"St. Martin de Porres." *Catholic Online.* http://www.catholic.org/saints/saint.php?saint_id=306.

Miscellaneous and Unpublished Works

Celebrating 30 Years of Educational Excellence at Martin University. DVD. Martin University. Indianapolis, 2007.

Hardin, Father Boniface. Interview by Alexander Jimenez and Ethan Ax, Indianapolis, 2006. Videocassette, tape 3. Property of Martin University, Indianapolis.

Kolentus, Robert. "The Origins of Martin University, 1920–Present." Indianapolis, unpublished book.

Index